KU-054-352

100
Italian
Dishes

100
Italian
Dishes

Edited by
Victoria Lloyd-Davies

Contents

NOTES
Standard spoon measurements are used in all recipes
1 tablespoon = one 15 ml spoon
1 teaspoon = one 5 ml spoon
All spoon measures are level.

Fresh herbs are used unless otherwise stated. If unobtainable, substitute a bouquet garni of the equivalent dried herbs, or use dried herbs instead but halve the quantities stated.
Ovens and grills (broilers) should be preheated to the specified temperature or heat setting.
For all recipes, quantities are given in metric, imperial and American measures. Follow one set of measures only, because they are not interchangeable.

**First published in hardcover in 1983 by
Octopus Books Limited
59 Grosvenor Street, London W1**

This edition published in 1983

© 1983 Octopus Books Limited

ISBN 0 7064 2024 1

Produced by Mandarin Publishers Limited
22a Westlands Road
Quarry Bay, Hong Kong

Printed in Hong Kong

Frontispiece: Stuffed Chicken Breasts (page 24)

Introduction

Italy is over nine hundred miles long and about two hundred miles wide. It takes a couple of days to travel from the northern Alps bordering Switzerland, to the southern tip of Sicily. The continuous changes in the landscape from the mountains and lakes in the north, to the hot and parched olive groves in the south, means the food is very varied along the way.

The area around Rome is probably the most sophisticated, and here hearty main courses are served with complicated sauces and lots of vegetable side dishes. This contrasts dramatically with Naples – the home of the first simple pizza. It is here that the tomatoes grow which are the basis of so many Italian dishes. Along the southern Adriatic coast stretch miles of almond and olive groves. The food here is much simpler and the pace much slower.

Pasta, of course, is served everywhere with regional variations. Spaghetti with tomato sauce originated from Naples, while around the "heel" of Italy, the local pasta is called orecchiette as they are shaped like little ears!

Fish is everywhere, too. Italy has one of the longest coastlines in Europe and the fish is so fresh that it is often just grilled with a little olive oil and served with wedges of Sicilian lemons. The fish soups and stews are delicious with all different kinds of fish included, from gigantic swordfish to tiny mussels. Anchovies are also often used in cooking; soak them first in milk to remove some of the saltiness.

All over Italy the women cook with olive oil. A good quality olive oil makes all the difference, so buy a large quantity and use it liberally. An abundance of tomatoes is necessary, too. They are much cheaper in Italy but you can bulk-buy tomatoes here at the end of the season, skin them and either freeze them whole or make tomato sauce and then freeze it in useful size portions. The alternative is to use canned Italian tomatoes.

The daily vegetable markets in Italy are wonderful as everything looks and tastes so fresh. As with pasta, the Italians cook their vegetables "al dente", leaving a little bite in them. Side salads abound from a plate of shredded lettuce and sliced tomato with an oil and vinegar dressing, to an artistic arrangement of colourful vegetables. The fruit is so good that few puddings as we know them appear on the menus. Instead a bowl of peaches, apricots and grapes kept cool in ice-cold water or a delicious selection of ice creams is more often served.

The variety of table cheeses seems endless – gorgonzola, dolcelatte and Bel Paese to name but a few. Italian cheeses may seem expensive to buy for cooking but there is nothing like freshly grated Parmesan or pecorino with pasta. Mozzarella is best for cooking but Bel Paese will 'melt and spread' too. Instead of ricotta, you can use cottage cheese, provided it is well drained.

Wine is the natural partner to all Italian food and every region in Italy has its own local wines in addition to the famous Valpolicelli, Chianti, Orvieto and Frascati.

This book has been written as the Italians would eat. Meals are a very important part of family life and are not hurried. The whole family, including the children, will sit down together for two hours or more and the children are welcome everywhere. They can get up between courses without upsetting their mother at home, or the waiter in a restaurant.

The meal in Italy starts with antipasti – a selection of meats and vegetables, or soups, or risotto. This is followed by the pasta course – spaghetti, tagliatelle, macaroni or a regional variation. Next comes the main course which is usually a small dish of fish, poultry or meat with vegetables or salads. Finally, the meal is rounded off with fresh fruit, ice cream or a simple dessert.

The Italians like to bake for special occasions. If you happen to be in Italy for Christmas, you will come across their sweet bread called Panettone. At Easter the traditional sweet bread is La Colomba or Easter Dove Bread. In Sicily, the wedding or festive cake is usually a light but highly decorated sponge accompanied with biscuits (cookies) which are handed round to all the guests. All these recipes are included as well as the traditional Zabaione.

At the end of the book is a chapter on what the French call 'Le Snack'. The Italians do not seem to eat much breakfast yet they will call in at a bar any time in the morning for a cup of strong black coffee – caffe, or black coffee with a dash of milk – cappuccino, and eat a sweet custard bun or a slice of Focaccia. After a large meal at midday, they might have a pizza and some wine in the evening.

Antipasti & Soups

Risotto Salami

METRIC/IMPERIAL	AMERICAN
25 g/1 oz butter	2 tablespoons butter
1 onion, chopped	1 onion, chopped
100 g/4 oz mushrooms, sliced	1 cup sliced mushrooms
1 red pepper, cored, seeded and diced	1 small red pepper, seeded and diced
1 small green pepper, cored, seeded and diced	1 small green pepper, seeded and diced
175 g/6 oz long grain rice	¾ cup long grain rice
450 ml/¾ pint chicken stock	2 cups chicken stock
salt and freshly ground pepper	salt and freshly ground pepper
113 g/4 oz pack salami, diced	¼ lb salami, diced
113 g/4 oz pack chicken roll, diced	¼ lb chicken roll, diced
100 g/4 oz peeled prawns	⅔ cup shelled shrimp
unpeeled prawns to garnish	unshelled shrimp for garnish

Melt the butter in a frying pan and fry the onion for 3 to 4 minutes. Add the mushrooms and peppers and cook for a further 3 minutes. Add the rice, stock and salt and pepper to taste. Bring the mixture to the boil, then lower the heat. Stir, then cover and simmer for 15 minutes.

When most of the liquid has been absorbed, add the meats and prawns to heat through. Garnish with unpeeled prawns (shrimp).
Cooking time: 30 minutes
Serves 6

Risotto Salami
(Photograph: Mattessons Meats)

Risotto Milanese

METRIC/IMPERIAL	AMERICAN
75 g/3 oz butter	⅓ cup butter
1 small onion, finely chopped	1 small onion, finely chopped
350 g/12 oz long grain rice	1¾ cups long grain rice
900 ml/1½ pints hot chicken stock or water	3¾ cups hot chicken stock or water
salt and freshly ground pepper	salt and freshly ground pepper
75 g/3 oz Cheddar cheese, finely grated	¾ cup finely grated Cheddar cheese

Melt two-thirds of the butter in a frying pan and cook the onion gently until tender. Add the rice and fry for a further 1 minute, stirring all the time to prevent burning.

Gradually pour in the hot stock or water. Bring to the boil, then lower the heat and cover and simmer for 15 minutes, or until rice is tender and liquid absorbed. Fluff up the mixture with a fork. Add salt and pepper to taste, the remaining butter and one-third of the cheese and stir gently. Serve remaining cheese separately.
Cooking time: 25 minutes
Serves 8

Risotto Marinara

METRIC/IMPERIAL	AMERICAN
2 tablespoons olive oil	2 tablespoons olive oil
2 cloves garlic, chopped	2 cloves garlic, chopped
100 g/4 oz long grain rice	½ cup long grain rice
1 × 250 g/9 oz can baby clams, drained	1 × 9 oz can baby clams, drained
1 × 250 g/9 oz can mussels in brine, drained	1 × 9 oz can mussels in brine, drained
300 ml/½ pint fish or chicken stock	1¼ cups fish or chicken stock
1 tablespoon coarsely chopped parsley	1 tablespoon coarsely chopped parsley

Heat the oil in a pan and fry the garlic until tender. Stir in the rice and continue to fry until the rice is golden brown, stirring all the time to prevent burning.

Stir in the clams, mussels and stock. Bring to the boil, then lower heat and cover and simmer for 15 minutes or until the rice is tender and liquid absorbed. Fluff up the mixture with a fork and stir in the chopped parsley.

Serve immediately with Italian bread sticks.
Cooking time: 25 minutes
Serves 4

Parma Ham and Melon

METRIC/IMPERIAL	AMERICAN
1 honeydew melon	1 honeydew melon
100 g/4 oz Italian smoked ham, thinly sliced	¼ lb Italian smoked ham, thinly sliced
freshly ground black pepper	freshly ground black pepper

Peel the melon, cut it into 8 wedges and carefully remove all the pips. Spread the slices of ham flat on a plate then wrap one slice of ham around each wedge of melon. Serve with freshly ground black pepper.

Alternatively, place the melon wedges on each plate and arrange 2 slices of ham beside the melon.
Serves 4

Antipasti

METRIC/IMPERIAL	AMERICAN
1 × 50 g/1¾ oz can anchovies	1 × 2 oz can anchovies
1 × 198 g/7 oz can tuna	1 × 7 oz can tuna
175 g/6 oz peeled prawns	1 cup shelled shrimp
1 × 120 g/4¼ oz can sardines	1 × 4¼ oz can sardines
100 g/4 oz Mortadella sausage, sliced	¼ lb Mortadella sausage, sliced
100 g/4 oz salami, thinly sliced	¼ lb salami, thinly sliced
3 hard-boiled eggs, quartered	3 hard-boiled eggs, quartered
½ cucumber, sliced	½ cucumber, sliced
3 tomatoes, quartered	3 tomatoes, quartered
1 × 400 g/14 oz can artichoke hearts	1 × 16 oz can artichoke hearts
lettuce	bibb lettuce
olive oil and wine vinegar	olive oil and wine vinegar

Arrange a selection of these foods on plates. Pour over a little oil and vinegar and serve.
Serves 4 to 6

Artichoke Salad

METRIC/IMPERIAL	AMERICAN
1 lettuce, shredded	1 bibb lettuce, shredded
1 × 400 g/14 oz can artichoke hearts, drained	1 × 16 oz can artichoke hearts, drained
100 g/4 oz Mortadella sausage, sliced	¼ lb Mortadella sausage, sliced
black olives	black olives
Dressing:	**Dressing:**
4 tablespoons olive oil	¼ cup olive oil
3 tablespoons lemon juice	3 tablespoons lemon juice
1 clove garlic, crushed	1 clove garlic, crushed
salt and freshly ground pepper	salt and freshly ground pepper

Arrange the lettuce on 4 plates. Place artichoke hearts, Mortadella and olives on the lettuce.

Whisk dressing ingredients in a bowl. Just before serving, pour the dressing over salad.
Serves 4

Minestrone

METRIC/IMPERIAL	AMERICAN
25 g/1 oz margarine	2 tablespoons margarine
2 onions, sliced	2 onions, sliced
1 or 2 cloves garlic, crushed (optional)	1 or 2 cloves garlic, crushed (optional)
2 rashers bacon, chopped	2 bacon slices, chopped
4 tomatoes, skinned and cut up	4 tomatoes, peeled and cut up
pinch of dried mixed herbs	pinch of dried mixed herbs
small glass of red wine	small glass of red wine
100 g/4 oz dried haricot beans, soaked overnight	½ cup dried haricot beans, soaked overnight
1.8 litres/3 pints stock or water	2 quarts stock or water
2 carrots, diced	2 carrots, diced
salt and freshly ground pepper	salt and freshly ground pepper
1 turnip, diced	1 turnip, diced
2 small potatoes, diced	2 small potatoes, diced
few sticks celery, chopped	few stalks celery, chopped
½ small cabbage, blanched and finely shredded	½ small cabbage, blanched and finely shredded
50 g/2 oz broken spaghetti	4 tablespoons broken spaghetti
5 tablespoons grated Parmesan cheese	5 tablespoons grated Parmesan cheese

Melt the margarine in a pan and lightly fry the onion and garlic if using. Add the bacon, tomatoes, herbs and red wine and bring to the boil. Add the drained haricot beans, cover with the stock or water and boil steadily for 1½ to 2 hours.

Add the carrots and salt and pepper to taste, then 15 minutes later add the turnip and potatoes. Cook for 10 minutes, then add the celery, cabbage and spaghetti and cook for a further 10 minutes.

Stir in 2 tablespoons grated Parmesan cheese and serve the extra Parmesan cheese separately.
Cooking time: 2 to 2½ hours
Serves 6 to 8

Florentine Tartlets

METRIC/IMPERIAL	AMERICAN
Pastry:	**Dough:**
225 g/8 oz plain flour	2 cups all-purpose flour
pinch of salt	pinch of salt
100 g/4 oz margarine	½ cup margarine
Filling:	**Filling:**
8 rashers streaky bacon	8 fatty bacon slices
100 g/4 oz packet frozen chopped spinach, thawed	¼ lb packet frozen chopped spinach, thawed
100 g/4 oz grated Parmesan cheese	1 cup grated Parmesan cheese
3 eggs	3 eggs
6 tablespoons milk	6 tablespoons milk
salt and freshly ground pepper	salt and freshly ground pepper

Sift the flour and salt into a bowl and rub (cut) in the margarine. Add enough water to make a stiff dough. Roll out dough thinly and cut into rounds, using a 7.5 cm (3 inch) cutter. Use the rounds to line 30 patty tins.

Remove the rind from the bacon and finely chop or mince the bacon. Lightly fry the bacon in a pan. Add the spinach and cook for a minute, then cool. Arrange the spinach mixture in the lined patty tins and top with the grated cheese. Beat the eggs, milk and salt and pepper together and carefully pour into pastry cases.

Cook in a preheated hot oven (220°C/425°F, Gas Mark 7) for about 15 minutes. Serve warm.
Cooking time: 20 minutes
Makes about 30

Lombardy Pea Soup

METRIC/IMPERIAL	AMERICAN
175 g/6 oz split peas	¾ cup split peas
salt and freshly ground pepper	salt and freshly ground pepper
50 g/2 oz margarine	¼ cup margarine
100 g/4 oz celery, diced	1 cup diced celery
175 g/6 oz potatoes, diced	1⅓ cups diced potatoes
2 onions, chopped	2 onions, chopped
1 × 113 g (4 oz) packet ham pâté	¼ lb ham pâté
900 ml/1½ pints hot stock	3¾ cups hot stock
1 tablespoon cornflour	1 tablespoon cornstarch
100 g/4 oz ham, diced	¼ lb ham, diced

Cover the peas with cold salted water and leave to soak overnight.

Next day, bring the peas to the boil in a pan, boil for 10 minutes and then simmer for 45 minutes.

Melt the margarine in a pan and sauté the celery, potatoes and onions for 5 minutes. Soften the pâté in a bowl, pour on the hot stock and mix well. Add to the vegetables and simmer for 25 minutes. Blend the cornflour (cornstarch) with a little cold water and add to the soup. Drain the peas and add to the soup. Simmer for a further 20 minutes.

Blend the soup in a blender or rub through a sieve until smooth. Add the ham and reheat the soup. Add salt and pepper to taste before serving.

Cooking time: about 2 hours
Serves 6

Italian Sausage Soup

METRIC/IMPERIAL	AMERICAN
1 tablespoon oil	1 tablespoon oil
1 onion, chopped	1 onion, chopped
1 clove garlic, crushed	1 clove garlic, crushed
2 carrots, diced	2 carrots, diced
1 stick celery, chopped	1 stalk celery, chopped
900 ml/1½ pints stock	3¾ cups stock
1 large potato, diced	1 large potato, diced
¼ cabbage, shredded	¼ cabbage, shredded
50 g/2 oz peas	⅓ cup peas
1 × 396 g/14 oz can tomatoes	1 × 16 oz can tomatoes
2 tablespoons tomato purée	2 tablespoons tomato paste
227 g/8 oz smoked pork sausage	½ lb smoked pork sausage
100 g/4 oz rice	½ cup rice
1 teaspoon dried oregano	1 teaspoon dried oregano
salt and freshly ground pepper	salt and freshly ground pepper

Heat the oil in a large pan, add the onion, garlic, carrots and celery and cook until vegetables are transparent. Add the stock, remaining vegetables and tomato purée (paste). Cover and cook over a low heat for 40 minutes.

Slice the smoked pork sausage into 1 cm (½ inch) pieces and add to the soup with the remaining ingredients. Cook for a further 15 to 20 minutes. Add salt and pepper to taste before serving.

Cooking time: 1 hour
Serves 6

Italian Sausage Soup; Lombardy Pea Soup
(Photograph: Mattessons Meats)

Italian Clear Soup

METRIC/IMPERIAL	AMERICAN
4 thin slices white bread	4 thin slices white bread
600 ml/1 pint consommé or clear chicken soup	2½ cups consommé or clear chicken soup
50 g/2 oz butter	¼ cup butter
4 eggs	4 eggs
1 tablespoon tomato purée	1 tablespoon tomato paste
1 tablespoon grated Parmesan cheese	1 tablespoon grated Parmesan cheese
1 tablespoon chopped parsley	1 tablespoon chopped parsley

Remove the crusts from the slices of bread and cut each slice into 4 squares.

Heat the soup to boiling. Meanwhile fry the bread in the butter until crisp on both sides. Pour the soup into 4 warm serving dishes and quickly break an egg into each. Add the bread squares and spoon on tomato purée (paste). Sprinkle over the cheese and parsley. Serve immediately.

Cooking time: 10 minutes
Serves 4

Note: alternatively the egg can be lightly poached in water, well drained and put into the serving dish before the soup is added.

Mussel Soup

METRIC/IMPERIAL	AMERICAN
3 tablespoons olive oil	3 tablespoons olive oil
1 onion, finely chopped	1 onion, finely chopped
1 stick celery, chopped	1 stalk celery, chopped
1 clove garlic, thinly sliced	1 clove garlic, thinly sliced
1 kg/2 lb tomatoes, skinned and chopped	4 cups peeled and chopped tomatoes
1 teaspoon dried oregano	1 teaspoon dried oregano
200 ml/⅓ pint white wine	⅞ cup white wine
200 ml/⅓ pint hot water	⅞ cup hot water
2.75 litres/5 pints mussels	12 cups mussels

Heat the oil in a large pan and cook the onion until soft but not brown. Add the celery and garlic and cook for 3 minutes. Add the tomatoes and oregano and cook, stirring, for 5 minutes. Pour over the white wine, cover and cook until the tomatoes are almost reduced to a pulp. Add the hot water and bring the soup to the boil. Take the soup off the heat and leave until required.

Scrub the mussels well and remove the beards. Discard any mussels that are open. Keep the closed mussels in cold water until required. Reheat the prepared soup and add all the mussels. Boil for 10 to 12 minutes, stirring occasionally, until all the mussels have opened. (Discard any mussels that do not open.)

Serve the cooked mussels in the soup. Place extra plates on the table for the discarded shells.

Cooking time: 1 hour
Serves 4

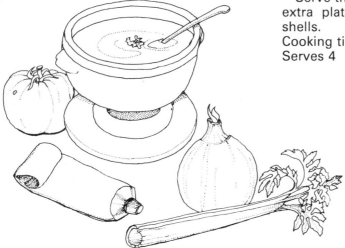

Genoese Fish Soup

METRIC/IMPERIAL	AMERICAN
2 tablespoons olive oil	2 tablespoons olive oil
1 onion, chopped	1 onion, chopped
1 clove garlic, crushed	1 clove garlic, crushed
3 sticks celery, sliced	3 stalks celery, sliced
50 g/2 oz streaky bacon, chopped	3 bacon slices, chopped
1 × 397 g/14 oz can tomatoes	1 × 16 oz can tomatoes
150 ml/¼ pint dry white wine	⅔ cup dry white wine
300 ml/½ pint fish or chicken stock	1¼ cups fish or chicken stock
½ teaspoon dried marjoram	½ teaspoon dried marjoram
salt and freshly ground black pepper	salt and freshly ground black pepper
450 g/1 lb monkfish, cod or coley	1 lb monkfish, cod or coley
100 g/4 oz peeled prawns	⅔ cup shelled shrimp
2 tablespoons chopped parsley to garnish	2 tablespoons chopped parsley for garnish

Heat the oil in a large pan and fry the onion, garlic, celery and bacon for 2 to 3 minutes. Add the tomatoes with their juice, wine, stock, marjoram and salt and pepper to taste. Simmer for 10 minutes.

Skin and dice the fish, add to the soup and cook for 5 minutes. Finally, add the prawns and simmer for a further 2 to 3 minutes. Season to taste and serve the soup hot, garnished with parsley.

Cooking time: 25 minutes
Serves 4 to 6

Tuscan Salad

METRIC/IMPERIAL	AMERICAN
1 lettuce	1 bibb lettuce
1 × 425 g/15 oz can cannellini beans	1 × 16 oz can cannellini beans
½ onion, thinly sliced	½ onion, thinly sliced
3 tomatoes, skinned and quartered	3 tomatoes, peeled and quartered
3 tablespoons olive oil	3 tablespoons olive oil
2 tablespoons wine vinegar	2 tablespoons wine vinegar
1 × 198 g/7 oz can tuna fish, drained	1 × 7 oz can tuna, drained

Arrange the lettuce on a serving dish. Drain the beans and mix with the onion and tomatoes. Whisk the oil and vinegar together, add to the bean mixture and toss together.

Arrange the salad on the lettuce and pile chunks of tuna on top.
Serves 4

Stracciatella

METRIC/IMPERIAL	AMERICAN
600 ml/1 pint consommé or clear chicken soup	2½ cups consommé or clear chicken soup
4 eggs	4 eggs
2 tablespoons grated Parmesan cheese	2 tablespoons grated Parmesan cheese
1 tablespoon semolina	1 tablespoon semolina
chopped parsley	chopped parsley
salt and freshly ground pepper	salt and freshly ground pepper

Heat the soup just to boiling point. Beat the eggs in a bowl with the cheese, semolina, some parsley, salt and pepper to taste and a little of the soup. Then whisk this mixture in a steady stream into the soup in the pan.

The finished soup will have a creamy, very lightly scrambled look.

Cooking time: 5 minutes
Serves 4

Pasta Dishes

Spaghetti Mozzarella

METRIC/IMPERIAL	AMERICAN
350 g/12 oz spaghetti	¾ lb spaghetti
3 tablespoons olive oil	3 tablespoons olive oil
salt and freshly ground black pepper	salt and freshly ground black pepper
100 g/4 oz butter	½ cup butter
1 clove garlic, finely chopped or crushed	1 clove garlic, finely chopped or crushed
4 tomatoes, cut into sections	4 tomatoes, cut into sections
75 g/3 oz black olives	½ cup black olives
175 g/6 oz Mozzarella or Bel Paese cheese, cubed	1 cup cubed Mozzarella or Bel Paese cheese
3 tablespoons chopped parsley	3 tablespoons chopped parsley

Cook the spaghetti in a large pan of boiling water with 1 tablespoon of oil and 1 teaspoon salt until just tender.

Meanwhile melt the butter in a small saucepan and stir over a gentle heat until it turns a nutty brown colour. Stir in the garlic and the remaining oil.

Drain the cooked spaghetti thoroughly and toss in the hot butter, together with the tomatoes, olives, cubed cheese, parsley and salt and pepper to taste. Serve immediately.

Cooking time: 15 minutes

Serves 4

Egg 'n' Spaghetti

METRIC/IMPERIAL	AMERICAN
225 g/8 oz spaghetti	½ lb spaghetti
1 tablespoon olive oil	1 tablespoon olive oil
1 teaspoon salt	1 teaspoon salt
100 g/4 oz streaky bacon, cooked and diced	¼ lb bacon slices, cooked and diced
50 g/2 oz mushrooms, sliced	½ cup sliced mushrooms
1 teaspoon dried oregano	1 teaspoon dried oregano
4 eggs, beaten	4 eggs, beaten
50 g/2 oz Cheddar cheese, grated	½ cup grated Cheddar cheese

Cook the spaghetti in a large pan of boiling water with 1 tablespoon oil and 1 teaspoon salt until tender. Drain and return to the pan.

Add the bacon, mushrooms, oregano and eggs. Cook until the eggs are just beginning to set. Add the cheese and cook for a few more minutes. Place in a serving dish and serve immediately.

Cooking time: 25 minutes

Serves 3 to 4

Spaghetti Mozzarella
(Photograph: Pasta Information Centre)

Egg Pasta Dough

METRIC/IMPERIAL	AMERICAN
225 g/8 oz plain flour	2 cups all-purpose
1 teaspoon salt	flour
1 tablespoon oil	1 teaspoon salt
2 eggs	1 tablespoon oil
	2 eggs

Turn the flour onto a work surface. Make a well in the centre and add the salt, oil and eggs. Work the mixture together to form a dough and knead for about 10 minutes until smooth.

Divide the dough into 4 pieces, place them on a plate and brush lightly with a little oil. Cover the plate with cling film (plastic wrap) and leave dough in a warm place for 1 hour to relax.

Remove a piece of dough from the warm place. Roll out on a well floured board as thinly as you can without tearing it. (The idea is to roll the dough so thinly that you can read through it!) Repeat with the other pieces of dough. As each piece of dough is rolled out, place it on one side of the work surface or if you have not very much room, place it over a tea towel resting on the back of a chair so that the dough can dry slightly. Do not leave the dough longer than half an hour or it will become dry at the edges and difficult to roll. When all the dough has been rolled out, take the first piece, place it on the work surface and sprinkle with a little flour, then roll the dough up rather likee a Swiss (jelly) roll. Cut into slices, 5 mm (¼ inch) thick to make tagliatelle or use the dough to make other pasta shapes. Unravel the slices and pile loosely on a plate.
Makes 350 g/12 oz pasta

Cooking Pasta

Allow 100-175 g/4-6 oz fresh homemade pasta per person, or 75-100 g/3-4 oz commercially made dry pasta.

Use the largest saucepan you have. Fill it three-quarters full with cold water, bring the water to the boil, then add 1 teaspoon of salt and 1 tablespoon of oil to every 2.25 litres/ 4 pints (10 cups) of water. Add the pasta, stirring, so that it does not stick together. When the water returns to the boil, reduce the heat so that the water is simmering fairly quickly.

Partially cover the pan and cook fresh pasta for about 5 minutes or dry pasta for about 15 minutes, but do follow packet instructions if using bought pasta as cooking times vary. The pasta is cooked when it is soft but it still has a little "bite" left. Drain the pasta in a colander and serve immediately.

Pasta with Egg and Cheese

Cook and drain 350 g/12 oz fresh homemade pasta. Add 50 g/2 oz (¼ cup) butter to the pan and add 120 ml/4 fl oz (½ cup) single (light) cream mixed with 3 egg yolks. Stir in the drained pasta, 175 g/6 oz (1½ cups) grated cheese and salt and pepper to taste. Stir well and serve hot.
Serves 2 to 3

Pasta with Cream

Cook and drain 350 g/12 oz fresh homemade pasta. Add 150 ml/¼ pint (⅔ cup) single (light) cream to the pan. Stir in the cooked pasta and season well with freshly ground black pepper. Stir well and serve immediately.
Serves 2 to 3

Spaghetti Marinara

METRIC/IMPERIAL	AMERICAN
225 g/8 oz spaghetti	½ lb spaghetti
1 tablespoon olive oil	1 tablespoon olive oil
1 teaspoon salt	1 teaspoon salt
25 g/1 oz margarine	2 tablespoons
25 g/1 oz plain flour	margarine
300 ml/½ pint milk	¼ cup all-purpose
1 teaspoon tomato	flour
purée	1¼ cups milk
salt and freshly	1 teaspoon tomato
ground pepper	paste
100 g/4 oz cooked	salt and freshly
peas	ground pepper
50 g/2 oz cooked	¾ cup cooked peas
sweetcorn	⅓ cup cooked whole
450 g/1 lb cooked and	kernel corn
flaked white fish,	1 lb cooked and
e.g. cod, whiting	flaked white fish,
	e.g. cod, whiting

Cook the spaghetti in a large pan of boiling water with 1 tablespoon oil and 1 teaspoon salt for about 10 minutes until just tender.

Meanwhile place the margarine, flour and milk in a small saucepan and bring to the boil, whisking continuously until smooth. Stir in remaining ingredients. Arrange the drained spaghetti in individual dishes and pour over the sauce.
Cooking time: 30 minutes
Serves 4 to 6

Spaghetti Carbonara

METRIC/IMPERIAL	AMERICAN
450 g/1 lb spaghetti	1 lb spaghetti
3 tablespoons olive oil	3 tablespoons olive oil
salt and freshly ground black pepper	salt and freshly ground black pepper
175 g/6 oz bacon, chopped	¾ cup chopped bacon
4 tablespoons stock	4 tablespoons stock
4 eggs	4 eggs
75 g/3 oz grated Parmesan cheese	¾ cup grated Parmesan cheese
75 g/3 oz mature Cheddar cheese, grated	¾ cup grated mature Cheddar cheese
1 teaspoon pasta seasoning	1 teaspoon pasta seasoning
6 tablespoons double cream	6 tablespoons heavy cream
½ teaspoon paprika	½ teaspoon paprika

Cook the spaghetti in a large pan of boiling water with 1 tablespoon of the oil and 1 teaspoon salt until just tender.

Meanwhile fry the chopped bacon in the remaining oil until crisp. Add the stock and cook briskly until the liquid has evaporated. Beat the eggs with the cheeses and pasta seasoning. Drain the cooked spaghetti and return it to the pan with the bacon. Add the egg and cheese miixture and stir quickly – there should be sufficient heat in the spaghetti to cook the eggs. Add the cream and paprika and stir for 30 seconds over a gentle heat.

Serve immediately, sprinkled with a little chopped parsley if liked.
Cooking time: 20 minutes
Serves 6

Spaghetti Bolognese

METRIC/IMPERIAL	AMERICAN
15 g/½ oz butter	1 tablespoon butter
1 onion, chopped	1 onion, chopped
225 g/8 oz minced lean beef	1 cup lean ground beef
1 clove garlic, crushed	1 clove garlic, crushed
4 tomatoes, skinned and diced	4 tomatoes, peeled and diced
1-2 teaspoons tomato purée(optional)	1-2 teaspoons tomato paste (optional)
2 teaspoons salt	2 teaspoons salt
pinch of pepper	pinch of pepper
150 ml/¼ pint stock	⅔ cup stock
15 g/½ oz flour, blended with a little cold water	2 tablespoons flour, blended with a little cold water
350-450 g (¾-1 lb) spaghetti	¾-1 lb spaghetti
1 tablespoon olive oil	1 tablespoon olive oil
Parmesan cheese to serve	Parmesan cheese to serve

Melt the butter in a pan. Fry the onion lightly, then add the minced meat and garlic. Add the tomatoes, tomato purée (paste) if using, 1 teaspoon salt, pepper and stock. Cover and simmer gently for about 40 minutes until the meat is tender, stirring from time to time. Add the blended flour and stir well.

Meanwhile cook the spaghetti in a large pan of boiling water with 1 tablespoon oil and 1 teaspoon salt for about 10 minutes. Drain well and serve in a hot dish with the meat sauce poured over. Sprinkle over Parmesan cheese.
Cooking time: 50 minutes
Serves 4

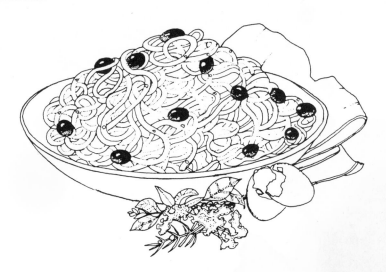

Cannelloni with Mushrooms

METRIC/IMPERIAL	AMERICAN
350 g/12 oz cannelloni	¾ lb cannelloni
1 tablespoon olive oil	1 tablespoon olive oil
1 teaspoon salt	1 teaspoon salt
Sauce:	**Sauce:**
300 ml/½ pint milk	1¼ cups milk
½ small bay leaf	½ small bay leaf
¼ teaspoon grated nutmeg	¼ teaspoon grated nutmeg
25 g/1 oz butter	2 tablespoons butter
25 g/1 oz plain flour	¼ cup all-purpose flour
Filling:	**Filling:**
1 chunk of bread	1 chunk of bread
1 tablespoon milk	1 tablespoon milk
1 hard-boiled egg, chopped	1 hard-boiled egg, chopped
225 g/8 oz mushrooms, chopped	2 cups chopped mushrooms
1 tablespoon chopped parsley	1 tablespoon chopped parsley
salt and freshly ground pepper	salt and freshly ground pepper
1 egg, beaten	1 egg, beaten
1 tablespoon cream	1 tablespoon cream
To finish:	**To finish:**
25 g/1 oz dry breadcrumbs	¼ cup dry bread crumbs
50 g/2 oz grated Parmesan cheese	½ cup grated Parmesan cheese

Cook the cannelloni in a large pan of boiling water with 1 tablespoon oil and 1 teaspoon salt until just tender. Drain and rinse well.

Meanwhile make the sauce: heat the milk, bay leaf and nutmeg in a pan and bring slowly to the boil. Remove from the heat, cover with a lid and leave the milk to infuse for 15 minutes. In a clean pan, melt the butter, stir in the flour and cook for 3 minutes. Strain the milk and gradually blend it into the pan. Bring the sauce to the boil, stirring continuously, then simmer for 2 to 3 minutes and adjust seasoning.

To make the filling: dip the bread in the milk and squeeze dry. Add the chopped egg, mushrooms and parsley to the bread, season with salt and pepper and add raw egg and cream. Carefully spoon the filling into the cannelloni tubes. Place them in a well buttered ovenproof dish, coat with the sauce and sprinkle with the breadcrumbs and cheese.

Cook in a preheated hot oven (220°C/425°F, Gas Mark 7) for 15 minutes until golden brown.
Cooking time: 45 minutes
Serves 4 to 6

Chicken and Bacon Lasagne

METRIC/IMPERIAL	AMERICAN
175 g/6 oz green or plain lasagne	6 oz green or plain lasagne
1 tablespoon olive oil	1 tablespoon olive oil
salt and freshly ground pepper	salt and freshly ground pepper
50 g/2 oz butter	¼ cup butter
1 onion, finely chopped	1 onion, finely chopped
25 g/1 oz plain flour	¼ cup all-purpose flour
300 ml/½ pint chicken stock	1¼ cups chicken stock
150 ml/¼ pint milk	⅔ cup milk
pinch of grated nutmeg	pinch of grated nutmeg
175 g/6 oz minced cooked bacon	¾ cup minced cooked bacon
225 g/8 oz cooked chicken, finely chopped	1 cup finely chopped cooked chicken
100 g/4 oz button mushrooms, sliced	1 cup sliced button mushrooms
juice of 1 lemon	juice of 1 lemon
200 ml/⅓ pint soured cream	⅞ cup sour cream
1 egg	1 egg
75 g/3 oz grated cheese	¾ cup grated cheese

Cook the sheets of lasagne in a large pan of boiling water with 1 tablespoon of oil and 1 teaspoon salt until tender. Drain the cooked pasta and lay the sheets of lasagne out on a well oiled surface, in a single layer.

Melt half the butter in a pan and sauté the onion. Stir in the flour and cook for 1 minute. Gradually add the stock and milk and bring to the boil, stirring, until the sauce has thickened. Add the grated nutmeg, salt and pepper to taste, minced bacon and chopped chicken.

Arrange the sauce and cooked lasagne in alternate layers in a greased ovenproof dish, starting with the sauce and finishing with lasagne. Cook the sliced mushrooms gently in the remaining butter with the lemon juice. Arrange the cooked mushrooms on top of the lasagne. Beat the soured cream with the egg and spoon evenly over the mushrooms. Sprinkle with the grated cheese. Cook in a moderately hot oven (190°C/375°F, Gas Mark 5) for 30 to 35 minutes until bubbling and golden.
Cooking time: 1 hour
Serves 6

Chicken and Bacon Lasagne (Photograph: Pasta Information Centre)

Lasagne Verdi

METRIC/IMPERIAL	AMERICAN
40 g/1½ oz butter	3 tablespoons butter
2 tablespoons oil	2 tablespoons oil
1 medium-sized onion, finely chopped	1 medium-sized onion, finely chopped
225 g/8 oz lean minced beef	½ lb lean minced beef
1 clove garlic, chopped	1 clove garlic, chopped
100 g/4 oz mushrooms, wiped and sliced	¼ lb mushrooms, wiped and sliced
300 ml/½ pint water	1¼ cups water
1 bay leaf	1 bay leaf
1 × 150 g/5 oz can tomato purée	1 × 5 oz can tomato paste
2 teaspoons sugar	2 teaspoons sugar
½ teaspoon basil or mixed herbs	½ teaspoon basil or mixed herbs
salt and freshly ground pepper	salt and freshly ground pepper
225 g/8 oz lasagne verdi	½ lb lasagne verdi
300 ml/½ pint cheese sauce	1¼ cups cheese sauce
50 g/2 oz Cheddar cheese, grated	½ cup grated Cheddar cheese

Heat the butter and 1 tablespoon oil in a pan and fry the onion slowly until golden brown and tender. Add beef and fry for a further 3 to 4 minutes, stirring all the time. Add the garlic and mushrooms to the pan with the water, bay leaf, tomato purée (paste), sugar, basil or mixed herbs and salt and pepper to taste. Bring slowly to the boil, stirring. Cover pan, lower heat and simmer gently for 30 minutes.

Remove lid and continue to cook for a further 20 to 30 minutes, stirring frequently, until sauce is thick and creamy and about half the liquid has evaporated.

Meanwhile cook the lasagne in a large pan of boiling water with 1 tablespoon oil and 1 teaspoon salt for about 20 minutes until tender, stirring often to prevent sticking. Arrange layers of cooked lasagne, meat sauce and cheese sauce in a 1 litre (2 pint) ovenproof dish, finishing with a layer of lasagne topped with cheese sauce. Sprinkle over the grated cheese. Cook the lasagne in a preheated moderate oven (180°C/350°F, Gas Mark 4) for 45 minutes to 1 hour. Serve hot.
Cooking time: 2 hours
Serves 4

Ravioli

METRIC/IMPERIAL	AMERICAN
Pasta:	**Pasta:**
750 g/1½ lb plain flour	6 cups all-purpose flour
pinch of salt	pinch of salt
2 large eggs, beaten	2 large eggs, beaten
2 tablespoons olive oil	2 tablespoons olive oil
175 ml/6 fl oz water	¾ cup water
Filling:	**Filling:**
225 g/8 oz Ricotta or cottage cheese	½ lb Ricotta or cottage cheese
350 g/12 oz cooked minced beef	¾ lb cooked minced beef
1 egg	1 egg
1 tablespoon chopped parsley	1 tablespoon chopped parsley
salt and freshly ground pepper	salt and freshly ground pepper
To serve:	**To serve:**
fresh tomato sauce (see page 44)	fresh tomato sauce (see page 44)
grated Parmesan cheese	grated Parmesan cheese

To make the pasta: sieve the flour and salt onto a board. Make a well in the centre and add eggs, olive oil and water. Carefully work flour into liquid, then knead pasta until smooth. Cut pasta in half. Roll out each half thinly into a strip, 30 × 45 cm (12 × 18 inches). Cut in half lengthwise.

To make the filling: mix together Ricotta or cottage cheese, cold beef, egg, parsley and salt and pepper to taste. Place 48 small teaspoonfuls of the mixture over one pasta strip, making 8 rows with 6 mounds of filling in each row. Dampen edges of pasta, then lay the other pasta strip over the top, sealing the edges well. Cut out ravioli using a pastry cutter and seal edges well. Chill. Repeat with other piece of pasta.

Drop ravioli into gently boiling water and cook for 10 to 15 minutes. Drain well and serve with fresh tomato sauce and Parmesan cheese.
Cooking time: 15 minutes
Serves 12 as a starter, or 8 as a main course

Tagliatelle with Tuna

METRIC/IMPERIAL	AMERICAN
350 g/12 oz tagliatelle	¾ lb tagliatelle
1 tablespoon olive oil	1 tablespoon olive oil
1 teaspoon salt	1 teaspoon salt
1 × 198 g/7 oz can tuna fish in oil	1 × 7 oz can tuna fish in oil
1 medium onion, chopped	1 medium onion, chopped
100 g/4 oz mushrooms, sliced	1 cup sliced mushrooms
salt and freshly ground pepper	salt and freshly ground pepper
150 ml/¼ pint double cream	⅔ cup heavy cream

Cook the tagliatelle in a large pan of boiling water with 1 tablespoon oil and 1 teaspoon salt until tender.

Meanwhile drain the oil from the tuna fish into a saucepan. Sauté the onion in the oil until tender, then add the mushrooms and cook until soft. Add salt and pepper to taste.

When the tagliatelle is cooked, drain well and return to the pan. Add the flaked tuna, onion and mushrooms. Pour in the cream and, over a low heat, mix all the ingredients together. Adjust seasoning and serve immediately.
Cooking time: 20 minutes
Serves 4

Gnocchi

METRIC/IMPERIAL	AMERICAN
300 ml/½ pint milk	1¼ cups milk
50 g /2 oz fine semolina	⅓ cup semolina flour
100g/4 oz Cheddar cheese, grated	1 cup grated Cheddar cheese
1 teaspoon salt	1 teaspoon salt
pinch of cayenne pepper and nutmeg	pinch of cayenne pepper and nutmeg
300 ml/½ pint fresh tomato sauce (see page 44)	1¼ cups fresh tomato sauce (see page 44)

Bring the milk to the boil and add the semolina all at once. Cook for several minutes, stirring vigorously all the time. Remove from the heat and stir in half the grated cheese and seasonings. Turn the mixture onto a large buttered and floured plate and spread evenly; leave to become quite cold.

Cut the mixture into neat pieces about 2.5 cm/1 inch square and place in a buttered flameproof dish. Sprinkle liberally with the remaining grated cheese and brown under a hot grill (broiler) for 15 to 20 minutes. Serve hot with fresh tomato sauce.
Cooking time: 25 minutes
Serves 3 to 4

Spinach Gnocchi

METRIC/IMPERIAL	AMERICAN
450 g/1 lb fresh spinach, or 1 × 400 g/14 oz packet frozen spinach	1 lb fresh spinach (or 1 × 14 oz packet frozen spinach)
100 g/4 oz Ricotta or cottage cheese	¼ lb Ricotta or cottage cheese
1 teaspoon salt	1 teaspoon salt
pinch of pepper	pinch of pepper
1 teaspoon grated nutmeg	1 teaspoon grated nutmeg
15 g/½ oz butter	1 tablespoon butter
25 g/1 oz grated Parmesan cheese	¼ cup grated Parmesan cheese
1 egg	1 egg
40 g/1½ oz plain flour	6 tablespoons all-purpose flour
To serve:	**To serve:**
25-50 g/1-2 oz butter, melted	2-4 tablespoons melted butter
25-50 g/1-2 oz grated Parmesan cheese	¼-½ cup grated Parmesan cheese

Cook the spinach in a very little boiling salted water in a covered pan. Drain, squeeze and chop finely. Sieve the Ricotta or cottage cheese. Return the spinach to the pan with the salt, pepper, nutmeg and butter. Add the Ricotta or cottage cheese. Stir over low heat for 5 minutes. Remove from the heat and beat in the cheese, egg and flour. Turn onto a plate and flatten. Leave to cool for several hours.

Using a little flour, shape the mixture into small croquettes. Have ready a large pan of boiling, salted water, drop the spinach gnocchi into it and cook for approximately 5 minutes. When they are cooked they will rise to the top. Drain the gnocchi in a colander. Toss carefully in melted butter and place in an ovenproof dish which has been lightly greased and dredged with Parmesan cheese. Dredge the gnocchi well with more Parmesan cheese and cook in a preheated moderate oven (180°C/350°F, Gas Mark 4) for 5 minutes.
Cooking time: 20 minutes
Serves 4

Poultry Dishes

Chicken Genoa

METRIC/IMPERIAL	AMERICAN
1 kg/2 lb oven-ready chicken	2 lb roasting chicken
salt and freshly ground pepper	salt and freshly ground pepper
2 tablespoons oil	2 tablespoons oil
25 g/1 oz butter	2 tablespoons butter
25 g/1 oz plain flour	¼ cup all-purpose flour
300 ml/½ pint chicken stock	1¼ cups chicken stock
1 small lemon	1 small lemon
2 egg yolks	2 egg yolks
2 tablespoons chopped parsley	2 tablespoons chopped parsley

Cut the chicken into four portions and season with salt and pepper. Heat the oil and butter in a large pan and gently fry the chicken pieces, turning them occasionally, for about 15 minutes until golden brown. Place the chicken on a plate and leave on one side.

Stir the flour into the pan and cook for 1 minute, then gradually stir in the chicken stock. Bring the sauce to the boil, stirring. Return the chicken to the pan, cover tightly and simmer for 30 to 40 minutes. Lift out the chicken, arrange on a dish and keep warm.

Pare the rind from the lemon and shred it, then squeeze the lemon juice. Skim off any surface fat from the sauce in the pan. Put the egg yolks and lemon juice into a small basin, add 2 tablespoons of the chicken sauce and beat lightly. Stir into the chicken sauce and heat, without boiling, until slightly thickened.

Adjust the seasoning of the sauce and pour it over the chicken. Serve garnished with the lemon shreds and chopped parsley.
Cooking time: about 1¼ hours
Serves 4
Chicken Genoa

Chicken Cacciatore

METRIC/IMPERIAL	AMERICAN
1 × 1.5 kg/3 lb chicken	1 × 3 lb chicken
3 tablespoons olive oil	3 tablespoons olive oil
2 onions, chopped	2 onions, chopped
1 clove garlic, chopped	1 clove garlic, chopped
450 g/1 lb tomatoes, skinned and chopped	1 lb tomatoes, peeled and chopped
225 g/8 oz mushrooms, sliced	2 cups sliced mushrooms
1 bay leaf	1 bay leaf
pinch of rosemary	pinch of rosemary
200 ml/⅓ pint red wine	⅞ cup red wine
salt and freshly ground pepper	salt and freshly ground pepper
sprigs of rosemary to garnish	rosemary sprigs for garnish

Divide the chicken into 4 portions. Heat the oil in a heavy pan. Add the onions and garlic and cook gently until golden. Remove the onion and garlic and turn up the heat, then brown the chicken on all sides in the oil. Replace the onion and add the tomatoes, mushrooms, herbs and wine.

Lower the heat, season well with salt and pepper to taste and cook very gently for about an hour, turning the chicken occasionally. Serve garnished with rosemary.
Cooking time: 1½ hours
Serves 4

Stuffed Chicken Breasts

METRIC/IMPERIAL	AMERICAN
4 chicken breasts	4 chicken breasts
salt and freshly ground black pepper	salt and freshly ground black pepper
4 thin slices ham	4 thin slices ham
4 thin slices Bel Paese cheese	4 thin slices Bel Paese cheese
4 asparagus spears, cooked	4 cooked asparagus spears
flour for dusting	flour for dusting
40 g/1½ oz butter	3 tablespoons butter
1 tablespoon olive oil	1 tablespoon olive oil
6 tablespoons Marsala	6 tablespoons Marsala
2 tablespoons chicken stock	2 tablespoons chicken stock
cooked or canned asparagus spears to garnish	cooked or canned asparagus spears for garnish

Lay the chicken breasts between damp pieces of greaseproof (waxed) paper and beat with a rolling pin until thin. Season the chicken with salt and pepper and lay a slice of ham on each portion, then a slice of cheese and an asparagus spear. Roll up each chicken breast carefully. If necessary, tie the rolls with cotton to keep in place, then dust with flour.

Heat 25 g/1 oz (2 tablespoons) butter and the oil in a frying pan and fry the chicken rolls over a very low heat for about 15 minutes, turning them frequently, until tender and golden. Remove the cotton and transfer the chicken to a hot serving dish and keep warm.

Add the Marsala, stock and remaining butter to the pan, bring to the boil and simmer for 3 to 4 minutes, stirring well. Spoon the sauce over the rolls and garnish with asparagus spears.
Cooking time: 20 minutes
Serves 4

Chicken Italienne

METRIC/IMPERIAL	AMERICAN
4 chicken portions	4 chicken portions
2 tablespoons plain flour, seasoned with salt and pepper	2 tablespoons all-purpose flour, seasoned with salt and pepper
2 tablespoons olive oil	2 tablespoons olive oil
1 large onion, chopped	1 large onion, chopped
1 clove garlic, crushed	1 clove garlic, crushed
1 × 397 g/14 oz can tomatoes	1 × 16 oz can tomatoes
2 tablespoons tomato purée	2 tablespoons tomato paste
200 ml/⅓ pint white wine	⅞ cup white wine
½ teaspoon dried thyme	½ teaspoon dried thyme
1 bay leaf	1 bay leaf
salt and freshly ground pepper	salt and freshly ground pepper

Coat the chicken portions with seasoned flour. Heat the oil in a pan and brown the chicken pieces on both sides; remove from pan. Fry the onion and garlic until soft, but not browned. Stir in any remaining flour, then add the tomatoes with their juice, tomato purée (paste), wine, thyme, bay leaf and salt and pepper to taste. Bring to the boil, stirring all the time, then add chicken, and simmer gently, covered, for about 1 hour, or until chicken is completely tender. Serve with new potatoes and a crisp green salad.
Cooking time: 1 hour 20 minutes
Serves 4

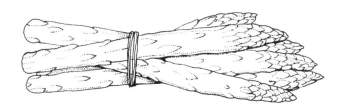

Chicken Tonnato

METRIC/IMPERIAL	AMERICAN
4 chicken breasts	4 chicken breasts
600 ml/1 pint chicken stock	2½ cups chicken stock
1 onion, halved	1 onion, halved
1 stick celery, roughly chopped	1 roughly chopped stalk celery
salt and freshly ground pepper	salt and freshly ground pepper
pinch of dried thyme	pinch of dried thyme
few parsley stalks	few parsley stalks
½ bay leaf	½ bay leaf
150 ml/¼ pint white wine (optional)	⅔ cup white wine (optional)
Sauce:	**Sauce:**
450 ml/¾ pint thick mayonnaise	2 cups thick mayonnaise
1 × 198 g/7 oz can tuna fish, drained	1 × 7 oz can tuna fish, drained
6 anchovy fillets, drained	6 anchovy fillets, drained
2 tablespoons lemon juice	2 tablespoons lemon juice
3 tablespoons drained capers	3 tablespoons drained capers
Garnish:	**Garnish:**
anchovy fillets	anchovy fillets
capers	capers
tomato slices	tomato slices

In a large pan, place chicken, stock, onion, celery, salt and pepper to taste, herbs, wine, if using, and enough water to cover; bring to the boil. Simmer very gently for 20 to 30 minutes until the chicken is tender and cooked. Remove chicken from the pan with a draining spoon and leave to cool.

In a blender, mix the mayonnaise, tuna fish, anchovy fillets, lemon juice and capers until smooth and well combined. Put the cooled chicken breasts on a serving dish and spoon sauce over them to cover. Garnish with anchovy strips, capers and tomato slices. Serve with a crisp green salad and any remaining sauce.

Cooking time: 30 minutes
Serves 4

Duck in Sweet-Sour Sauce

METRIC/IMPERIAL	AMERICAN
1 × 2-2.25 kg/4½-5 lb duckling	1 × 4½-5 lb duckling
salt and freshly ground pepper	salt and freshly ground pepper
25 g/1 oz plain flour	¼ cup all-purpose flour
2 tablespoons olive oil	2 tablespoons olive oil
2 large onions, thinly sliced	2 large onions, thinly sliced
¼ teaspoon ground cloves	¼ teaspoon ground cloves
600 ml/1 pint well flavoured duckling stock, prepared from the giblets	2½ cups well flavored duckling stock, prepared from the giblets
2 tablespoons finely chopped fresh mint or 2 level teaspoons dried mint	2 tablespoons finely chopped fresh mint or 2 teaspoons dried mint
75 g/3 oz sultanas	½ cup raisins
50 g/2 oz sugar	¼ cup sugar
4 tablespoons water	4 tablespoons water
2 tablespoons wine vinegar	2 tablespoons wine vinegar
sprigs of mint to garnish	sprigs of mint for garnish

Wipe the duckling inside and out with kitchen paper towels. Season well with salt and pepper and dredge well with the flour.

Heat the oil in a large flameproof casserole and gently fry the onions for 2 to 3 minutes until soft. Add the duckling and cook, turning as necessary, until browned all over. Sprinkle with ground cloves. Pour in the strained stock, bring slowly to the boil then reduce heat, cover with a lid and simmer gently for 1½ hours or until tender. Carefully remove duck from pan, divide into 4 portions with kitchen scissors or a sharp knife and arrange on a serving dish; keep hot.

Skim the fat from the liquid in the pan then stir in the mint and sultanas (raisins). Meanwhile heat the sugar in a small heavy pan with the water until it turns deep golden brown. Stir this into the mint sauce, taking care as it will splutter a little at first. Stir in the vinegar and simmer for 5 to 10 minutes without a lid until the sauce is reduced to a syrupy consistency. If liked, place the duckling under a hot grill for 2 to 3 minutes to brown. Coat with the prepared sauce and garnish with sprigs of mint.

Cooking time: 2 hours
Serves 4

Duckling with Olives

METRIC/IMPERIAL	AMERICAN
1 × 2-2.25 kg/4½-5 lb duckling	1 × 4½-5 lb duckling
salt	salt
Sauce:	**Sauce:**
50 g/2 oz streaky bacon, chopped	¼ cup chopped bacon slices
1 carrot, thinly sliced	1 carrot, thinly sliced
1 small onion, finely chopped	1 small onion, finely chopped
1 clove garlic, crushed	1 clove garlic, crushed
1 stick celery, chopped	1 stalk celery, chopped
25 g/1 oz plain flour	¼ cup all-purpose flour
300 ml/½ pint well-flavoured duckling stock, prepared from the giblets	1¼ cups well-flavored duckling stock, prepared from the giblets
2 tablespoons tomato purée	2 tablespoons tomato paste
½ teaspoon dried basil	½ teaspoon dried basil
salt and freshly ground pepper	salt and freshly ground pepper
150 ml/¼ pint white wine	⅔ cup white wine
2 large green olives, stoned and sliced	2 large green pitted olives, sliced
12 black olives, stoned and sliced	12 pitted ripe olives, sliced
Garnish:	**Garnish:**
shredded lemon rind	shredded lemon rind
few whole green and black olives	few whole green and ripe olives

Wash the duckling and pat dry inside and out with kitchen paper towels. Prick the skin all over with a fork and rub with salt. Place the duckling, breast uppermost, on a wire rack in a roasting pan. Roast the duckling without covering, in the centre of a preheated moderate oven (350°F/180°C, Gas Mark 4) allowing 30 minutes per lb.

Meanwhile prepare the sauce: heat 2 tablespoons of duckling dripping (taken from the roasting duck) in a saucepan, add the bacon and fry for 2 to 3 minutes until lightly browned. Add the carrot, onion, garlic and celery and fry for a further 5 minutes. Sprinkle in the flour, mix well and continue frying until lightly browned. Remove from the heat and gradually blend in the strained stock and tomato purée (paste). Stir in the basil. Return to the heat and stir until the sauce thickens. Season well with salt and freshly ground pepper to taste. Reduce heat and simmer very gently for 1 hour, stirring from time to time to prevent sticking.

Press the prepared sauce through a sieve into a clean, small roasting tin. Blend in the white wine and olives. Cut the roast duckling into 4 portions with kitchen scissors and add to the pan, spooning a little sauce over each portion. Return to a preheated moderately hot oven (200°C/400°F, Gas Mark 6), and cook for 20 minutes or until heated through.

Arrange the duckling on a hot serving dish with the sauce. Sprinkle with lemon rind and garnish with green and black olives.
Cooking time: about 3 hours
Serves 4

Lombardy Stew

METRIC/IMPERIAL	AMERICAN
8 tablespoons olive oil	8 tablespoons olive oil
1 carrot, chopped	1 carrot, chopped
1 onion, chopped	1 onion, chopped
750 g/1½ lb tomatoes, skinned and chopped	1½ lb tomatoes, peeled and chopped
1 bay leaf	1 bay leaf
600 ml/1 pint stock	2½ cups stock
sugar and salt to taste	sugar and salt to taste
40 g/1½ oz plain flour	6 tablespoons all-purpose flour
3 tablespoons milk	3 tablespoons milk
1 rabbit, jointed or 4 rabbit portions	1 rabbit, jointed or 4 rabbit portions

Heat 4 tablespoons of the oil in a large flameproof dish and fry the carrot and onion for a few minutes. Add tomatoes, bay leaf and stock. Cover and simmer for 15 to 20 minutes. Strain and season with sugar and salt to taste.

Mix flour and milk together until smooth and add to the tomato sauce. Bring to the boil, stirring.

Fry rabbit joints in remaining oil, drain and add to the sauce. Cover and cook gently for about 1½ hours or until the rabbit is tender.
Cooking time: 2 hours
Serves 4

Duckling with Olives
(Photograph: British Duck Advisory Bureau)

Turkey Fillets Limone

METRIC/IMPERIAL	AMERICAN
4 turkey fillets or escalopes	4 turkey cutlets
salt and freshly ground pepper	salt and freshly ground pepper
75 g/3 oz butter or margarine	1/3 cup butter or margarine
2 onions, finely chopped	2 onions, finely chopped
100 g/4 oz button mushrooms, sliced	1 cup sliced button mushrooms
40 g/1½ oz plain flour	6 tablespoons all-purpose flour
450 ml/¾ pint chicken stock	2 cups chicken stock
grated rind and juice of 1 lemon	grated rind and juice of 1 lemon
1-2 tablespoons chopped parsley	1-2 tablespoons chopped parsley
50 g/2 oz chopped gherkins (optional)	1/3 cup chopped gherkins (optional)
4 tablespoons double cream (optional)	¼ cup heavy cream (optional)

Season the turkey with salt and pepper. Melt the butter or margarine in a frying pan and gently fry the onions until soft. Add the turkey and fry lightly on each side to seal then remove from the pan.

Add the mushrooms to the pan and fry for a minute or so, then stir in the flour and cook for a further minute. Add the stock and lemon rind and juice and bring to the boil. Stir in the parsley and gherkins, if using, and replace the turkey. Cover pan and simmer gently for about 30 minutes, turning once or twice, until tender. Adjust seasoning, stir in the cream, if using, and serve.

Cooking time: 50 minutes
Serves 4

Turkey with Capers

METRIC/IMPERIAL	AMERICAN
2 turkey breast steaks, halved lengthwise	2 turkey breasts, halved lengthwise
salt and freshly ground pepper	salt and freshly ground pepper
4 tablespoons oil	¼ cup oil
40 g/1½ oz plain flour	6 tablespoons all-purpose flour
300 ml/½ pint single cream	1¼ cups light cream
150 ml/¼ pint white wine	2/3 cup white wine
1 tablespoon finely grated lemon rind	1 tablespoon finely grated lemon rind
1 teaspoon fresh thyme or ½ teaspoon dried thyme	1 teaspoon fresh thyme or ½ teaspoon dried thyme
¼ teaspoon dried marjoram	¼ teaspoon dried marjoram
2 tablespoons capers	2 tablespoons capers
Garnish:	**Garnish:**
few strips of thinly pared lemon rind	few strips of thinly pared lemon rind
watercress	watercress

Rub the turkey with salt and pepper. Heat the oil in a pan over a moderate heat and fry the turkey gently for 4 to 5 minutes on each side until lightly browned. Remove and place in an ovenproof dish.

Stir the flour into the pan juices and cook for 1 minute, then gradually stir in the cream and wine. Bring the sauce to just below boiling point, stirring continuously, then lower the heat and simmer for 2 minutes. Add the remaining ingredients and pour over the turkey. Cover and cook in a preheated moderate oven (180°C/350°F, Gas Mark 4) for 15 minutes or until the turkey is tender. Taste and adjust the seasoning, if necessary.

Garnish with strips of lemon rind and watercress and serve with plain boiled rice or baked jacket potatoes and a salad or coleslaw.

Cooking time: 30 minutes
Serves 4

Italian Roast Turkey

METRIC/IMPERIAL	AMERICAN
1 × 4 kg/9 lb turkey	1 × 9 lb turkey
15 g/½ oz butter	1 tablespoon butter
1 tablespoon oil	1 tablespoon oil
Stuffing:	**Stuffing:**
50 g/2 oz canned prunes, stoned	½ cup prunes, pitted
450 g/1 lb peeled chestnuts (or 1 large can chestnuts)	1 lb peeled chestnuts (or 1 large can chestnuts)
6 tablespoons stock or milk	6 tablespoons stock or milk
225 g/8 oz sausagemeat	½ lb sausagemeat
liver from the turkey	liver from the turkey
1 large onion	1 large onion
25 g/1 oz butter	2 tablespoons butter
salt and pepper	salt and pepper
3-4 tablespoons white wine	3-4 tablespoons white wine
Braise:	**Braise:**
40 g/1½ oz butter	3 tablespoons butter
2 onions, sliced	2 onions, sliced
2 carrots, sliced	2 carrots, sliced
3 sticks celery, chopped	3 stalks celery, chopped
3 rashers bacon, chopped	3 bacon slices, chopped
2 cloves garlic	2 cloves garlic
450 ml/¾ pint red wine	2 cups red wine
300 ml/½ pint turkey stock	1¼ cups turkey stock
6 peppercorns	6 peppercorns
1 sprig rosemary or 2 teaspoons dried rosemary	1 sprig rosemary or 2 teaspoons dried rosemary
2 bay leaves	2 bay leaves

To make the stuffing: roughly chop the prunes. If using fresh chestnuts, cook them in boiling water for 5 minutes and then remove the skins. Cook them for a further 30 minutes in the stock or milk then drain and chop them roughly. (If using canned chestnuts just drain and chop roughly.) Mix the prunes and chestnuts with the sausagemeat. Chop the liver and the onion. Fry in the butter for a few minutes and then add to the other stuffing ingredients. Add seasoning to taste and wine and mix well; allow to cool. Stuff the turkey and sew up with fine string.

To make the braise: melt the butter in a large flameproof dish or pan and fry the onions, carrots, celery, bacon and garlic for 2 minutes. Pour over the wine and stock and add seasonings.

Rub the turkey with the butter and oil and place in the dish. Cover and cook in a preheated moderate oven (180°C/350°F, Gas Mark 4) for 3½ hours.

Serve the turkey on a large platter surrounded with the vegetables.

Cooking time: 4½ hours
Serves 10

Turkey Saltimbocca

METRIC/IMPERIAL	AMERICAN
4 turkey breast fillets	4 turkey breast fillets
a little flour	a little flour
4 slices lean ham	4 slices lean ham
50 g/2 oz Cheddar cheese, grated	½ cup grated Cheddar cheese
50 g/2 oz grated Parmesan cheese	½ cup grated Parmesan cheese
oil for frying	oil for frying
3 tomatoes, skinned and finely diced	3 tomatoes, peeled and finely diced
50 g/2 oz walnuts, roughly chopped	½ cup roughly chopped walnuts
chopped parsley to garnish	chopped parsley for garnish

Using a wooden rolling pin or a steak bat, flatten the turkey breasts on a well floured surface until very thin and double the size – take care to keep them well floured as they break easily if sticky. Alternatively, put the turkey breasts between two sheets of oiled foil and beat until thin. Dust each of the breasts with flour then place a slice of ham on each, trimming the edges to fit the turkey. Mix the cheeses together and sprinkle a little over the ham, and then roll up with the turkey meat on the outside.

Heat the oil in a pan and fry each roll until golden brown on the outside and cooked through. Place on a flameproof serving dish or grill tray and sprinkle with the remaining cheese, then with the diced tomato and walnuts. Grill for a few minutes until the cheese melts. Garnish with chopped parsley and serve.

Cooking time: 20 minutes
Serves 4

Fish & Meat Dishes

Mullet in a Parcel

METRIC/IMPERIAL	AMERICAN
2 tablespoons olive oil	2 tablespoons olive oil
2 cloves garlic, finely chopped	2 cloves garlic, finely chopped
½ teaspoon dried fennel	½ teaspoon dried fennel
1 red pepper, cored, seeded and sliced	1 red pepper, seeded and sliced
1 green pepper, cored, seeded and sliced	1 green pepper, seeded and sliced
2 onions, sliced	2 onions, sliced
450 g/1 lb courgettes, sliced	1 lb zucchini, sliced
225 g/8 oz mushrooms, sliced	2 cups sliced mushrooms
4 red mullet	4 red mullet
salt and freshly ground pepper	salt and freshly ground black pepper

Heat the oil in a large frying pan. Gently sauté the garlic, fennel and vegetables for 5 minutes until tender.

Meanwhile slit each fish along the belly. Snip off the fins and wash the fish well, removing the gut. Keep the fish whole.

Place each mullet on a piece of foil and season with salt and pepper. Place the vegetables around each fish and fold over the foil to make 4 individual parcels. Cook in a preheated moderately hot oven (190°C/375°F, Gas Mark 5) for 30 minutes.

To serve the fish, open the foil on each parcel and remove the eyes from the fish.
Cooking time: 35 minutes
Serves 4

Mullet in a Parcel
(Photograph: Sea Fish Kitchen)

Fritto Misto Mare

METRIC/IMPERIAL	AMERICAN
oil for deep frying	oil for deep frying
750 g/1½ lb mixed fish (squid, sole fillets, sprats, scampi)	1½ lb mixed fish (squid, sole fillets, smelts, jumbo prawns)
a little plain flour, seasoned with salt and pepper	a little all-purpose flour, seasoned with salt and pepper
lemon wedges to garnish	lemon wedges for garnish

Heat the oil in a deep fryer to 190°C/375°F. Clean the squid and cut the bodies into thin rings; cut the sole into thin strips. Coat all the fish, including the squid tentacles, in seasoned flour.

Deep fry the fish in small batches for 2 to 3 minutes until crisp and golden brown. Drain on kitchen paper towels and serve garnished with lemon wedges.
Cooking time: 30 minutes
Serves 4 to 6

Italian Fish Stew

METRIC/IMPERIAL	AMERICAN
5 tablespoons olive oil	5 tablespoons olive oil
1 onion, sliced	1 onion, sliced
1 clove garlic, crushed	1 clove garlic, crushed
225 g/8 oz carrots, peeled and cut into strips	½ lb carrots, peeled and cut into strips
1 × 397 g/14 oz can tomatoes	1 × 16 oz can tomatoes
100 g/4 oz black olives	¾ cup ripe olives
1 bay leaf	1 bay leaf
salt and freshly ground black pepper	salt and freshly ground black pepper
4 slices white bread	4 slices white bread
4 × 175 g/6 oz cod steaks or 750 g/ 1½ lb cod, coley or huss, cut into chunks	4 × 6 oz cod steaks or 1½ lb cod, coley or huss
300 ml/½ pint mussels, scrubbed and beards removed	1¼ cups mussels, scrubbed and beards removed
2 tablespoons chopped parsley	2 tablespoons chopped parsley

Melt 2 tablespoons oil in a pan and fry the onion, garlic and carrots for 2 to 3 minutes. Add the tomatoes with their juice, olives, bay leaf and season with a little salt and some black pepper. Simmer for 15 minutes.

Meanwhile cut four circles from the slices of bread and fry in the remaining oil until crisp and golden. Drain on kitchen paper towels and keep warm.

Add the fish to the stew and cook for 5 minutes. Finally add the cleaned mussels and cook for another 4 to 5 minutes or until the shells open. Discard any mussels which do not open. Adjust the seasoning and remove the bay leaf.

Put a croûte of fried bread in the bottom of each large soup bowl, place cod on top. Gently pour over the vegetables and mussels. Serve sprinkled with parsley.
Cooking time: 35 minutes
Serves 4

Pork Slices with Yogurt Sauce

METRIC/IMPERIAL	AMERICAN
750 g/1½ lb pork tenderloin, thinly sliced	1½ lb pork tenderloin, thinly sliced
2 tablespoons plain flour, seasoned with salt and pepper	2 tablespoons all-purpose flour, seasoned with salt and pepper
1 egg, beaten	1 egg, beaten
50 g/2 oz fresh white breadcrumbs	1 cup soft white bread crumbs
4 tablespoons olive oil	4 tablespoons olive oil
1 hard-boiled egg, roughly chopped	1 hard-boiled egg, roughly chopped
150 ml/¼ pint plain yogurt	⅔ cup plain yogurt
1 lemon, sliced	1 lemon, sliced

Coat the pork with the seasoned flour. Dip the pork in the beaten egg and then coat with breadcrumbs.

Heat the oil in a frying pan and fry the pork slices until golden brown. Drain, arrange on a serving dish and keep hot. Mix together the egg and yogurt. Heat through gently and pour over the pork. Garnish with the slices of lemon.
Cooking time: 5 to 10 minutes
Serves 4

Neapolitan Pork Chops

METRIC/IMPERIAL	AMERICAN
2 tablespoons olive oil	2 tablespoons olive oil
1 clove garlic, crushed	1 clove garlic, crushed
4 thick pork chops	4 center cut pork chops
salt and freshly ground pepper	salt and freshly ground pepper
3 tablespoons white wine	3 tablespoons white wine
3 tablespoons tomato purée	3 tablespoons tomato paste
1 green pepper, cored, seeded and chopped	1 green pepper, seeded and chopped
350 g/12 oz mush- rooms, sliced	3 cups sliced mushrooms

Heat the oil in a large frying pan, brown the garlic and then discard it. In the same pan, brown the chops well on both sides. Sprinkle with a good pinch of salt and a little pepper.

Mix together the wine and tomato purée (paste) and add to the pan. Add the green pepper and mushrooms to the pan and cook, covered, over a low heat for 45 minutes or until chops are cooked.
Cooking time: 50 minutes
Serves 4

Beef Steaks with Lemon

METRIC/IMPERIAL	AMERICAN
4 thin rump steaks	4 thin top round
1 lemon, cut into	steaks
quarters	1 lemon, cut into
Marinade:	quarters
4 tablespoons white	**Marinade:**
wine	4 tablespoons white
2 tablespoons olive	wine
oil	2 tablespoons olive
juice of 1 lemon	oil
salt and freshly	juice of 1 lemon
ground pepper	salt and freshly
1 clove garlic,	ground pepper
crushed	1 clove garlic,
½ teaspoon dried	crushed
oregano	½ teaspoon dried
	oregano

Using a rolling pin or steak bat, flatten the steaks. Mix all the marinade ingredients together and pour over the meat in a glass bowl. Leave to marinate in a cool place for 2 hours.

Drain off the marinade and cook meat under a heated grill for 5 minutes. Turn steaks and cook for a further 5 minutes. Serve with lemon quarters.
Cooking time: 10 minutes
Serves 4

Roman Beef Stew

METRIC/IMPERIAL	AMERICAN
4 tablespoons olive	¼ cup olive oil
oil	3 slices bacon,
3 rashers bacon,	chopped
chopped	1½ lb boneless beef
750 g/1½ lb stewing	for stew, cut into
steak, cut into	cubes
cubes	5 tablespoons red
5 tablespoons red	wine
wine	1 clove garlic,
1 clove garlic,	crushed
crushed	1 onion, chopped
1 onion, chopped	1 × 10.9 oz jar pasta
1 × 10.9 oz jar	sauce
Napoletana pasta	salt and freshly
sauce	ground black
salt and freshly	pepper
ground black	1 cup diced carrots
pepper	2 large diced potatoes
225 g/8 oz carrots,	1 cup sliced zucchini
diced	
2 large potatoes,	
diced	
100 g/4 oz courgettes,	
sliced	

Heat the oil in a large pan and cook the bacon. Remove the bacon from pan. Brown the meat in the oil. Add the wine, garlic, onion, pasta sauce and salt and pepper to taste. Cover and simmer for 1½ hours.

Add the carrots and potatoes and cook for another 40 minutes. Add the courgettes (zucchini) and chopped bacon and heat through for a final 10 minutes.
Cooking time: 2½ hours
Serves 4

Osso Buco

METRIC/IMPERIAL	AMERICAN
1.5-1.75 g/3-4 lb shin of veal	3-4 lb boneless veal for stew
50 g/2 oz plain flour	½ cup all-purpose flour
6 tablespoons olive oil	6 tablespoons olive oil
1 onion, thinly sliced	1 onion, thinly sliced
1 carrot, grated	1 carrot, grated
1 stick celery, chopped	1 stalk celery, chopped
8 tomatoes, skinned and chopped	8 tomatoes, peeled and chopped
1 tablespoon tomato purée	1 tablespoon tomato paste
150 ml/¼ pint white wine	⅔ cup white wine
150 ml/¼ pint chicken stock	⅔ cup chicken stock
salt and freshly ground pepper	salt and freshly ground pepper
Garnish:	**Garnish:**
finely chopped parsley	finely chopped parsley
1 clove garlic, chopped	1 clove garlic, chopped
finely grated rind of 1 small lemon	finely grated rind of 1 small lemon

Ask the butcher to saw the veal shin into 7.5 cm/ 3 inch pieces. Coat the meat in the flour. Heat the oil in a large pan. Add the veal pieces, a few at a time, and fry until well browned. Remove to a plate.

Add the onion, carrot and celery to the remaining oil in the pan and fry slowly until soft but not brown. Stir in the tomatoes, tomato purée (paste), wine, stock and salt and pepper to taste and bring to the boil. Replace the veal, lower the heat and cover pan. Simmer very gently for 1½ to 2 hours until tender. Turn onto a warm dish.

Mix together the garnish ingredients and sprinkle them over the veal.
Cooking time: 2 to 2½ hours
Serves 4

Escalope Milanese

METRIC/IMPERIAL	AMERICAN
6 × 100 g/4 oz veal escalopes	6 × 4 oz veal cutlets
50 g /2 oz plain flour	½ cup all-purpose flour
2 eggs, beaten	2 eggs, beaten
salt	salt
75 g/3 oz fresh breadcrumbs	1½ cups soft bread crumbs
300 ml/½ pint olive oil	1¼ cups olive oil
2 lemons, cut into wedges	2 lemons, cut into wedges

Trim the veal and make a few cuts around the edges. Beat the veal well with a rolling pin to flatten it. Sift the flour onto a plate. Mix the beaten egg with some salt on a second plate, and put the breadcrumbs on a third one. Dip the veal first into the flour and shake off the surplus. Then dip the veal into the beaten eggs and finally into the breadcrumbs. Do not press down the crumbs, just shake off surplus.

Heat the oil in a frying pan and fry two veal escalopes at a time until golden brown on each side (about 2 minutes each side). Drain on kitchen paper towels and keep hot while cooking the other escalopes. Serve with lemon wedges.
Cooking time: 30 minutes
Serves 6

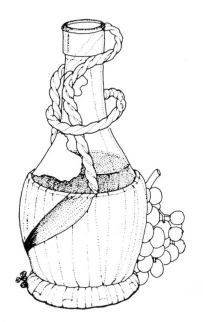

Escalope Milanese
(Photograph: pan from the Columbine range by Pointerware)

Lamb Chops Rosa Marina

METRIC/IMPERIAL	AMERICAN
50 g/2 oz butter, softened	¼ cup softened butter
4 lamb chops	4 lamb chops
chopped fresh rosemary	chopped fresh rosemary
freshly ground black pepper	freshly ground black pepper

Spread a little of the butter on each of the lamb chops. Sprinkle with a little rosemary and black pepper. Arrange the chops on a grill (broiler) pan and cook for 7 minutes. Turn the chops over and cook for a further 7 minutes.

Serve the lamb chops with new potatoes and green beans.

Cooking time: 15 minutes
Serves 4

Lamb Kebabs Roma

METRIC/IMPERIAL	AMERICAN
½ shoulder lamb, boned	1 lb boneless lamb for stew
1 small green pepper, blanched, cored and seeded	1 small green pepper, blanched and seeded
2 lambs' kidneys, skinned, cored and halved	2 lamb kidneys, skinned, cored and halved
2 medium onions, blanched and quartered	2 medium onions, blanched and quartered
4 tomatoes, halved	4 tomatoes, halved
4 mushrooms, halved	4 mushrooms, halved
Marinade:	**Marinade:**
2 tablespoons olive oil	2 tablespoons olive oil
2 tablespoons wine vinegar	2 tablespoons wine vinegar
pinch of mixed herbs	pinch of mixed herbs
pinch of sugar	pinch of sugar
pinch of dry mustard	pinch of dry mustard
1 clove garlic, crushed	1 clove garlic, crushed
salt and freshly ground black pepper	salt and freshly ground black pepper

Cut the meat into cubes and put into a glass bowl. Mix the marinade ingredients thoroughly together and pour over the lamb. Leave for several hours in a cool place, turning occasionally.

Cut the green pepper into 8 portions. Thread the lamb, kidneys, onion, green pepper, tomatoes and mushrooms onto 4 skewers and baste with the marinade. Place under a hot grill (broiler), turning frequently until cooked through. Serve with rice and a crisp green salad.

Cooking time: 15 to 20 minutes
Serves 4

Tuscany Lamb Casserole

METRIC/IMPERIAL	AMERICAN
1 best end neck of lamb	1 lamb rib rack
4 tablespoons olive oil	¼ cup olive oil
1 bay leaf	1 bay leaf
salt and freshly ground pepper	salt and freshly ground pepper
150 ml/¼ pint white wine	⅔ cup white wine
1 red pepper, cored, seeded and sliced	1 red pepper, seeded and sliced
1 clove garlic, chopped	1 clove garlic, chopped
1 tablespoon chopped parsley	1 tablespoon chopped parsley

Weigh the lamb and calculate the cooking time, allowing 25 minutes per pound weight.

Place the lamb in a casserole with half the oil and bay leaf and season lightly with salt and pepper. Cover and cook in a preheated moderately hot oven (190°C/375°F, Gas Mark 5), basting and turning the meat occasionally. When it begins to brown, add the white wine and continue basting. Cook the lamb for the calculated time.

Ten minutes before the end of cooking time, fry the sliced red pepper, chopped garlic and chopped parsley together in the remaining oil. Pour all the juices from the casserole over the pepper mixture, removing the bay leaf. Pour this mixture back over the meat. Serve the lamb, divided into cutlets.

Cooking time: 1½ hours
Serves 4

Liver Pomodoro

METRIC/IMPERIAL
25 g/1 oz margarine
350 g/12 oz lambs'
liver, cut into 1 cm/
½ inch strips
4 rashers back bacon,
chopped
25 g/1 oz plain flour
300 ml/½ pint stock
8-12 spring onions,
washed and
trimmed
1 × 200 g/7 oz can
tomatoes
salt and freshly
ground pepper

AMERICAN
2 tablespoons
margarine
¾ lb lamb liver, cut
into ½ inch strips
4 slices bacon,
chopped
¼ cup all-purpose
flour
1¼ cups stock
8-12 scallions,
washed and
trimmed
1 × 7 oz can tomatoes
salt and freshly
ground pepper

Melt the margarine in a pan and fry the liver
and bacon. Remove from pan and drain on
kitchen paper towels. Add the flour to
remaining fat in pan and cook for 1 minute.

Remove from the heat and gradually stir in
the stock. Return to the heat and bring to the
boil, stirring. Return liver and bacon to the pan,
add spring onions (scallions), tomatoes with
their juice and salt and pepper to taste. Simmer
gently for 15 minutes, stirring occasionally.
Serve with rice.
Cooking time: 30 minutes
Serves 4

Sweetbreads Napoletana

METRIC/IMPERIAL
750 g/1½ lb calves'
sweetbreads,
cleaned and sliced
2 tablespoons olive
oil
300 ml/½ pint milk
4 slices of toast
75 g/3 oz mixed
Parmesan and
Cheddar cheese,
grated
salt and paprika
pepper
50 g/2 oz mushrooms,
sliced
25 g/1 oz margarine

AMERICAN
1½ lb veal
sweetbreads,
cleaned and sliced
2 tablespoons olive
oil
1¼ cups milk
4 slices of toast
¾ cup grated
Parmesan and
Cheddar cheese,
mixed
salt and paprika
pepper
½ cup sliced
mushrooms
2 tablespoons
margarine

Sauté the sweetbread slices in the oil. Put
1 tablespoon milk into an ovenproof dish and
lay in the slices of toast.

Mix the remaining milk with the cheese, salt
and paprika pepper and spread over the toast.
Lay the sautéed sweetbreads on top and add
the sliced mushrooms. Put flakes of margarine
over the top. Cover and cook in a preheated
moderate oven (180°C/350°F, Gas Mark 4) for 20
minutes. Serve the sweetbreads with creamed
potatoes and carrots.
Cooking time: 30 minutes
Serves 4

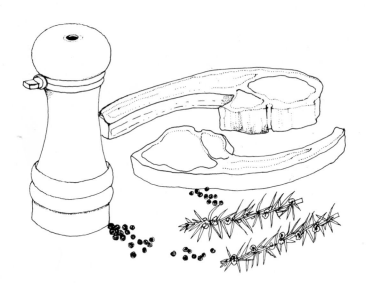

Salads & Vegetable Dishes

Peperonata Flan

METRIC/IMPERIAL	AMERICAN
Pastry:	**Dough:**
100 g/4 oz plain flour	1 cup all-purpose flour
pinch of salt	pinch of salt
50 g/2 oz margarine	¼ cup margarine
2 tablespoons water	2 tablespoons water
Filling:	**Filling:**
50 g/2 oz butter	¼ cup butter
100 g/4 oz aubergine, sliced	1 cup sliced eggplant
100 g/4 oz courgettes, sliced	1 cup sliced zucchini
100 g/4 oz tomatoes, skinned and chopped	½ cup tomatoes, peeled and chopped
1 onion, chopped	1 onion, chopped
1 small green pepper, seeded and sliced	1 small green pepper, seeded and sliced
100 g/4 oz bacon, chopped	½ cup chopped bacon slices
salt and freshly ground pepper	salt and freshly ground pepper
100 g/4 oz Cheddar cheese, grated	1 cup grated Cheddar cheese

Sift the flour and a pinch of salt into a bowl and rub (cut) in the margarine until the mixture resembles fine breadcrumbs. Add enough water to mix to a fairly stiff dough. Roll out the dough on a lightly floured surface and use to line a 19 cm/7½ inch foil flan dish.

Melt the butter in a pan and fry all the vegetables and bacon until just tender. Add salt and pepper to taste and leave until cold. Spoon the vegetables into the flan and cover the top of the flan with foil. Cook in a preheated moderately hot oven (200°C/400°F, Gas Mark 6) for 15 minutes. Remove foil, pile grated cheese on top of vegetables and return to the oven for a further 15 minutes, or until cheese has melted and is golden brown. Serve hot.
Cooking time: 40 minutes
Serves 4

Peperonata Flan
(Photograph: Bacofoil Information Service)

Italian Meat Salad

METRIC/IMPERIAL	AMERICAN
25 g/1 oz finely chopped parsley	¾ cup finely chopped parsley
25 g/1 oz finely chopped spring onions	¼ cup finely chopped scallions
1 clove garlic, finely chopped	1 clove garlic, finely chopped
2 tomatoes, skinned and chopped	2 tomatoes, peeled and chopped
2 teaspoons finely chopped capers	2 teaspoons finely chopped capers
25 g/1 oz fresh white breadcrumbs	½ cup soft white bread crumbs
120 ml/4 fl oz olive oil	½ cup olive oil
4 tablespoons lemon juice	4 tablespoons lemon juice
salt and freshly ground pepper	salt and freshly ground pepper
350 g/12 oz sliced cooked cold meat	¾ lb sliced cooked cold meat
4 tablespoons single cream	¼ cup light cream

Place the chopped parsley, spring onions (scallions), garlic, tomatoes and capers in a bowl. Stir in the breadcrumbs, oil, lemon juice and salt and pepper to taste.

Arrange the meat on a large flat plate and spoon the sauce over. Cover and leave in a cool place for at least 1 hour. Swirl the cream over the dressing just before serving.
Serves 4 to 6

Napoletana Flan

METRIC/IMPERIAL	AMERICAN
Pastry:	**Dough:**
100 g/4 oz plain flour	1 cup all-purpose flour
pinch of salt	pinch of salt
50 g/2 oz margarine	¼ cup margarine
2 tablespoons water	2 tablespoons water
Filling:	**Filling:**
25 g/1 oz butter	2 tablespoons butter
1 clove garlic, crushed	1 clove garlic, crushed
25 g/1 oz plain flour	¼ cup all-purpose flour
150 ml/¼ pint chicken stock	⅔ cup chicken stock
1 × 227 g/8 oz can tomatoes, drained	1 × 8 oz can tomatoes, drained
salt and freshly ground pepper	salt and freshly ground pepper
100 g/4 oz Mozzarella or Bel Paese cheese, thinly sliced	¼ lb Mozzarella or Bel Paese cheese, thinly sliced
Garnish:	**Garnish:**
1 × 50 g/1¾ oz can anchovy fillets, drained	1 × 2 oz can anchovy fillets, drained
sliced stuffed olives	sliced stuffed olives

Sift the flour and salt into a bowl, rub (cut) in the margarine until the mixture resembles fine breadcrumbs. Add enough water to make a stiff dough. Roll out the dough and use to line a 20 cm/8 inch flan dish. Prick the base with a fork, then cook in a preheated hot oven (220°C/425°F, Gas Mark 7) for 15 to 20 minutes. Leave to cool.

Melt the butter in a pan and lightly fry the garlic. Add the flour and cook for a minute, stirring. Remove from the heat and gradually stir in the stock. Return to the heat, bring to the boil, stirring, and continue to cook for a few minutes. Add the tomatoes and salt and pepper to taste. Mix well and turn into the flan case. Arrange the sliced cheese on top and garnish with anchovy fillets and olives.

Cook the flan in a preheated moderately hot oven (200°C/400°F, Gas Mark 6) for about 20 minutes, until the cheese has melted. Serve hot.

Cooking time: 45 minutes
Serves 4

Corn and Pasta Salad

METRIC/IMPERIAL	AMERICAN
225 g/8 oz pasta shells	2 cups pasta shells
4 tablespoons olive oil	4 tablespoons olive oil
1 teaspoon salt	1 teaspoon salt
1 tablespoon vinegar	1 tablespoon vinegar
1 × 198 g/7 oz can tuna fish	1 × 7 oz can tuna fish
1 teaspoon grated lemon rind	1 teaspoon grated lemon rind
1 clove garlic, crushed	1 clove garlic, crushed
2 sticks celery, sliced	2 stalks celery, sliced
1 onion, thinly sliced	1 onion, thinly sliced
1 × 198 g/7 oz can sweetcorn, drained	1 × 7 oz can whole kernel corn, drained
salt and freshly ground black pepper	salt and freshly ground black pepper
50 g/2 oz French beans	50 g/2 oz green beans
50 g/2 oz mushrooms, sliced	½ cup sliced mushrooms
25 g/1 oz butter	2 tablespoons butter
chopped parsley to garnish	chopped parsley for garnish

Cook the pasta shells in boiling water with 1 tablespoon oil and 1 teaspoon salt until just tender. Drain and cool. Put the remaining oil and vinegar into a bowl. Add the oil from the tuna, lemon rind, garlic and stir well. Add the flaked tuna, celery, onion, corn and pasta shells and toss together, adding salt and pepper to taste; chill.

Cut the beans into 2.5 cm/1 inch pieces and cook in boiling salted water until tender; cool. Lightly fry the mushrooms in butter and allow to cool. Transfer the salad to a serving dish. Arrange the sliced mushrooms and beans on top. Garnish with chopped parsley.

Cooking time: 35 minutes
Serves 4 to 6

Sardinian Seafood Salad

METRIC/IMPERIAL	AMERICAN
225 g/8 oz wholewheat tagliatelle	½ lb wholewheat tagliatelle
50 g/2 oz button mushrooms	½ cup button mushrooms
25 g/1 oz butter	2 tablespoons butter
100 g/4 oz cooked and shelled mussels	½ cup cooked and shelled mussels
100 g/4 oz peeled prawns	⅔ cup shelled shrimp
1 × 50 g/1¾ oz can anchovies, drained	1 × 2 oz can anchovies, drained
3 tomatoes, cut into wedges	3 tomatoes, cut into wedges
120 ml/4 fl oz Italian dressing* (see recipe right)	½ cup Italian dressing (see recipe right)
Garnish:	**Garnish:**
2 tablespoons chopped parsley	2 tablespoons chopped parsley
2 tablespoons grated Parmesan cheese	2 tablespoons grated Parmesan cheese
4 lemon twists	4 lemon twists

Cook the tagliatelle as directed on the packet; drain thoroughly.

Meanwhile lightly fry the mushrooms in the butter, then drain on kitchen paper towels. While still warm, mix the pasta with the mussels, prawns (shrimp) and anchovies. Add the mushrooms and tomatoes and pour over the dressing. Mix thoroughly and turn into a serving dish. Chill in the refrigerator for 2 hours.

When ready to serve, sprinkle over the chopped parsley and Parmesan cheese and garnish with lemon twists.
Cooking time: 20 minutes
Serves 4 to 6

Genoese Salad

METRIC/IMPERIAL	AMERICAN
1 × 425 g/15 oz can cannellini beans	1 × 16 oz can cannellini beans
100 g/4 oz thinly sliced salami	¼ lb thinly sliced salami
225 g/8 oz Lancashire cheese	1½ cups crumbled Lancashire cheese
olive oil	olive oil
salt and freshly ground black pepper	salt and freshly ground black pepper

Drain the beans well and mix them in a salad bowl with the salami. Crumble the cheese over the top. Pour a little oil over and sprinkle with salt and pepper. Serve chilled with crusty bread.
Serves 4

Italian Dressing

METRIC/IMPERIAL	AMERICAN
5 tablespoons olive oil	5 tablespoons olive oil
1 tablespoon lemon juice	1 tablespoon lemon juice
1 tablespoon wine vinegar	1 tablespoon wine vinegar
1 clove garlic, crushed	1 clove garlic, crushed
salt and freshly ground black pepper	salt and freshly ground black pepper
2 anchovy fillets, crushed, or ½ teaspoon dried oregano	2 anchovy fillets, crushed, or ½ teaspoon dried oregano

Mix together the oil, lemon juice, vinegar, garlic and salt and pepper to taste. Either add the crushed anchovy fillets or the oregano. Allow the dressing to stand for 1 hour for the flavours to blend.
Serves 4

Italian Ratatouille

METRIC/IMPERIAL	AMERICAN
450 g/1 lb aubergines, sliced	1 lb eggplant, sliced
salt and freshly ground pepper	salt and freshly ground pepper
4 tablespoons olive oil	¼ cup olive oil
1 large onion, sliced	1 large onion, sliced
1 green pepper, cored, seeded and sliced	1 green pepper, seeded and sliced
450 g/1 lb courgettes, sliced	1 lb zucchini, sliced
4 tomatoes, skinned and sliced	4 tomatoes, peeled and sliced

Sprinkle the sliced aubergines (eggplant) with salt. Leave for about 1 hour and then drain off water; dry. Heat 2 tablespoons oil in a frying pan and lightly fry the onion. Add remaining 2 tablespoons oil and green pepper and courgettes (zucchini). Continue frying gently, turning occasionally. Add aubergines (eggplant) and continue cooking, then add the tomatoes and salt and pepper to taste. Cook for about 40 minutes.
Cooking time: 1 hour
Serves 6
Note: it is a good idea to prepare a large quantity of ratatouille when the vegetables are cheaper in the autumn, then freeze it in small and large freezer trays until required.

Aubergine (Eggplant) and Mozzarella Layer

METRIC/IMPERIAL	AMERICAN
450 g/1 lb aubergines	1 lb eggplant
salt	salt
a little flour	a little flour
1 egg, beaten	1 egg, beaten
100 g/4 oz fresh white breadcrumbs	2 cups soft white bread crumbs
oil for frying	oil for frying
100 g/4 oz Mozzarella cheese, sliced	¼ lb sliced Mozzarella cheese
600 ml/1 pint fresh tomato sauce (see recipe on page 44)	2½ cups fresh tomato sauce (see recipe on page 44)
15 g/½ oz grated Parmesan cheese	2 tablespoons grated Parmesan cheese
green pepper rings to garnish	green pepper rings for garnish

Peel the aubergines (eggplant) and slice them thinly lengthwise. Sprinkle with a little salt and leave for 1 hour. Wash and dry well. Dip the slices in flour, then beaten egg and finally in the breadcrumbs. Fry in small batches in hot oil until crisp. Drain on kitchen paper towels.

Put a layer of aubergines (eggplant) in a 2 litre/3½ pint (9 cup) casserole. Cover with a layer of Mozzarella cheese then spoon over some tomato sauce. Continue to fill the casserole in layers, finishing with a layer of aubergines (eggplant). Sprinkle over the Parmesan cheese. Cover the casserole with the lid and cook in a preheated moderate oven (180°C/350°F, Gas Mark 4) for 30 minutes. Remove the lid for the last 5 minutes to brown the top.
Cooking time: 1 hour
Serves 4 to 6

Cauliflower Insalata

METRIC/IMPERIAL	AMERICAN
1 large cauliflower, cut into florets	1 large cauliflower, cut into florets
salt and freshly ground pepper	salt and freshly ground pepper
50 g/2 oz green olives, halved and stoned	⅓ cup pitted green olives
6 anchovy fillets, chopped	6 anchovy fillets, chopped
juice of ½ lemon	juice of ½ lemon
5 tablespoons olive oil	5 tablespoons olive oil
1 tablespoon chopped parsley	1 tablespoon chopped parsley
1 tablespoon capers	1 tablespoon capers

Cook the cauliflower in boiling salted water for about 5 minutes – it should still be quite crisp. Drain and set aside to cool.

Place the cauliflower, olives and anchovies in a salad bowl and mix together. Whisk together the lemon juice, oil and salt and pepper to taste and add to the salad. Add the parsley and toss together. Chill the salad and sprinkle with the capers before serving.
Serves 4

Aubergine (Eggplant) and Mozzarella Layer (Photograph: Country style casserole by Corning Ltd, the manufacturers of Pyrex)

Stuffed Aubergines (Eggplant)

METRIC/IMPERIAL	AMERICAN
2 medium-sized aubergines	2 medium-sized eggplant
½ teaspoon salt	½ teaspoon salt
olive oil	olive oil
1 × 50 g/1¾ oz can anchovies, drained and chopped	1 × 2 oz can anchovies, drained and chopped
1 tablespoon chopped parsley	1 tablespoon chopped parsley
1 tablespoon grated onion	1 tablespoon minced onion
1 tomato, skinned and chopped	1 tomato, peeled and chopped
50 g/2 oz fresh breadcrumbs	1 cup soft bread crumbs
pepper	pepper

Wash the aubergines (eggplant) and remove the stalks, then cut in half lengthwise. Cut around each aubergine half 5mm/¼ inch from the skin and then criss-cross cut the surface lightly to ensure even cooking. Sprinkle with salt and 2 teaspoons of olive oil. Place in a greased ovenproof dish and cook in a preheated moderately hot oven (190°C/375°F, Gas Mark 5) for 15 to 20 minutes, until the centre is almost cooked.

Meanwhile mix together the anchovies, parsley, onion, tomato, breadcrumbs and pepper to taste for the stuffing. Scoop out the flesh from the centre of the cooked aubergines (eggplant), chop up and add to the stuffing. Fill the aubergine (eggplant) cases, mounding the stuffing. Brush with oil and return to the oven for a further 15 minutes. Serve hot with a main dish.

Cooking time: 35 minutes
Serves 4

Fresh Tomato Sauce

METRIC/IMPERIAL	AMERICAN
6 tablespoons olive oil	6 tablespoons olive oil
2 onions, chopped	2 onions, chopped
2 cloves garlic, chopped	2 cloves garlic, chopped
450 g/1 lb tomatoes, skinned and chopped	2 cups peeled and chopped tomatoes
1 stick celery, thinly sliced	1 stalk celery, thinly sliced
150 ml/¼ pint chicken stock	⅔ cup chicken stock
salt and freshly ground pepper	salt and freshly ground pepper
pinch of oregano or chopped parsley	pinch of oregano or chopped parsley
pinch of sugar	pinch of sugar

Heat the oil in a pan and fry the onions and garlic until lightly brown. Add the tomatoes and celery and simmer gently for 5 minutes. Add the stock, salt and pepper to taste, herbs and sugar, and continue to cook slowly for a further 10 minutes.

Cooking time: 20 minutes
Makes 900 ml/1½ pints (3¾ cups)
Note: it is a good idea to prepare a large quantity of fresh tomato sauce when tomatoes are cheaper in the autumn, then freeze the sauce in small and large freezer bags until required.

For a hotter sauce, cook one finely chopped chilli pepper with the tomatoes. This hot tomato sauce is especially good served with spaghetti.

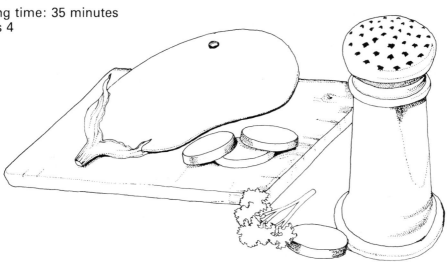

Italian-Style Cauliflower

METRIC/IMPERIAL	AMERICAN
1 large cauliflower	1 large cauliflower
salt	salt
25 g/1 oz butter	2 tablespoons butter
1 medium-sized onion, chopped	1 medium-sized onion, chopped
1 clove garlic, finely chopped	1 clove garlic, finely chopped
350 g/12 oz tomatoes, skinned and chopped	1½ cups peeled and chopped tomatoes
1 tablespoon chopped parsley	1 tablespoon chopped parsley
25 g/1 oz grated Parmesan cheese	¼ cup grated Parmesan cheese
Cheese sauce:	**Cheese sauce:**
50 g/2 oz butter	¼ cup butter
50 g/2 oz plain flour	½ cup all-purpose flour
600 ml/1 pint milk	2½ cups milk
pinch of salt and cayenne pepper	pinch of salt and cayenne pepper
175 g/6 oz Cheddar cheese, finely grated	1½ cups finely grated Cheddar cheese

Cook the cauliflower in boiling salted water until tender. Melt the butter in a pan and cook the onion and garlic gently. Add the tomatoes and parsley.

To make the cheese sauce: melt the butter in a pan, add the flour and cook for 1 minute. Remove from the heat and gradually stir in the milk. Return to the heat and bring to the boil, stirring. Cook for 1 minute and then remove from the heat. Add salt and pepper to taste and Cheddar cheese, and stir until cheese has melted.

Drain the cauliflower well and place in an ovenproof dish. Spoon the tomato mixture over the cauliflower and coat with the cheese sauce. Sprinkle with Parmesan cheese and brown under a hot grill (broiler).
Cooking time: 40 minutes
Serves 4 to 6

Courgettes (Zucchini) and Tomato Medley

METRIC/IMPERIAL	AMERICAN
750 g/1½ lb courgettes, sliced	3 cups sliced zucchini
1 tablespoon salt	1 tablespoon salt
2 tablespoons olive oil	2 tablespoons olive oil
1 small onion, chopped	1 small onion, chopped
1 clove garlic, finely chopped	1 clove garlic, finely chopped
450 g/1 lb tomatoes, skinned and sliced	2 cups peeled and sliced tomatoes
2 tablespoons wine vinegar	2 tablespoons wine vinegar
1 tablespoon lemon juice	1 tablespoon lemon juice
1 tablespoon caster sugar	1 tablespoon sugar
salt and freshly ground pepper	salt and freshly ground pepper

Sprinkle the courgettes (zucchini) with the salt and toss lightly. Leave to drain for 1 hour. Shake the courgettes in a cloth to dry. Heat the oil in a large frying pan. Add the onion and garlic and cook for 2 to 3 minutes. Add the courgettes and cook gently, stirring occasionally, for about 10 to 15 minutes. When the courgettes are soft, add the tomatoes. Stir in the vinegar, lemon juice and sugar. Add salt and pepper to taste and heat through for about 5 minutes.
Cooking time: 25 minutes
Serves 4

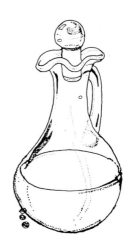

Cakes & Desserts

Nougat Refrigerator Cake

METRIC/IMPERIAL	AMERICAN
200 g/7 oz unsalted butter, softened	⅞ cup softened unsalted butter
200 g/7 oz caster sugar	⅞ cup sugar
50 g/2 oz cocoa	½ cup unsweetened cocoa
50 g/2 oz drinking chocolate	½ cup sweetened cocoa
1 egg	1 egg
1 egg yolk	1 egg yolk
100 g/4 oz Nice biscuits	¼ lb sweet crackers
100 g/4 oz chopped almonds	1 cup chopped almonds
2 tablespoons brandy	2 tablespoons brandy
Decoration:	Decoration:
150 ml/¼ pint double cream, whipped	⅔ cup heavy cream, whipped
sugar flowers	sugar flowers

Beat the butter and sugar together until creamy, add the sifted cocoa and drinking chocolate and mix it well into the buttercream. Beat the egg and egg yolk together and beat them into the cocoa mixture. Crush the biscuits (crackers) with a rolling pin and add the crumbs to the chocolate mixture with the chopped almonds. Mix well. Add the brandy and mix again very thoroughly.

Line a lightly greased 23 cm/9 inch cake tin with greaseproof (waxed) paper. Spoon the biscuit crumb mixture into the pan, then press it down and flatten it with a palette knife. Refrigerate the cake for at least 3 hours. Turn the cake onto a round dish and cover with cream, then decorate with sugar flowers.
Serves 10

Nougat Refrigerator Cake
(Photograph: Tate & Lyle)

Pignolata Strufoli

METRIC/IMPERIAL	AMERICAN
150 g/5 oz plain flour	1¼ cups all-purpose flour
¼ teaspoon salt	¼ teaspoon salt
2 eggs	2 eggs
oil for frying	oil for frying
100 g/4 oz caster sugar	½ cup sugar
7 tablespoons clear honey	7 tablespoons honey
25 g/1 oz flaked almonds	¼ cup slivered almonds

Sift 100 g/4 oz (1 cup) flour and the salt onto a board and make a well in the centre. Break eggs into the centre of the flour. Knead together gently, gradually adding enough of the remaining flour to make a medium soft dough – the texture will become softer after kneading.

Roll out the dough to a 5 mm/¼ inch thickness. Cut into 5 mm/¼ inch wide strips. Twist two strands together and cut into pieces 1 cm/½ inch long.

Heat the oil and, when very hot, add the pieces of dough, a few at a time. Stir with a wooden spoon for 1 or 2 minutes. Remove from the oil and drain.

Blend the sugar and honey in a pan over the heat for 5 minutes, but do not boil. Add the cooked "twists" to the mixture, stirring with a wooden spoon until they are completely covered with syrup. Arrange like two bunches of grapes on two plates. Decorate with almonds to form leaves.
Cooking time: 30 minutes
Serves 8

Almond Soufflé

METRIC/IMPERIAL	AMERICAN
Almond purée:	**Almond purée:**
175 g/6 oz flaked almonds	1½ cups slivered almonds
300 ml/½ pint milk	1¼ cups milk
15 g/½ oz caster sugar	1 tablespoon sugar
Soufflé:	**Soufflé:**
300 ml/½ pint milk	1¼ cups milk
2 drops vanilla essence	2 drops vanilla
15 g/½ oz butter	1 tablespoon butter
50 g/2 oz strong plain white flour	½ cup strong all-purpose white flour
6 egg yolks (1 to be kept separate)	6 egg yolks (1 to be kept separate)
8 egg whites	8 egg whites
65 g/2½ oz caster sugar	5 tablespoons sugar
4 macaroons	4 macaroons
200 ml/⅓ pint Amaretto di Saronno	⅞ cup Amaretto di Saronno
sieved icing sugar, to decorate	sifted confectioners' sugar, to decorate

To make the almond purée: put the almonds, milk and sugar in a saucepan and simmer gently for 40 minutes. When cooked, pass through a fine sieve (or use a blender or food processor) and blend until the mixture is fine.

Grease and flour four 7.5 cm/3 inch individual soufflé dishes.

To prepare the soufflé: put two-thirds of the milk in a heavy pan with the vanilla and butter and bring to the boil. Remove from the heat and stir in the rest of the milk, the flour and one egg yolk. Heat again until the mixture becomes thick, and then whisk briskly. Add the 5 remaining egg yolks and cook for another 2 minutes until the mixture begins to stiffen. Whisk the egg whites until stiff and whisk in the sugar.

Soak the macaroons with 5 tablespoons/⅓ cup Amaretto di Saronno and put one macaroon, cut into cubes, into each soufflé dish. Blend the soufflé mixture with the almond purée and remaining Amaretto di Saronno. Carefully fold in the stiffly beaten egg whites. Spoon this mixture into the soufflé dishes. Cook in a preheated hot oven (220°C/425°F, Gas Mark 7) for 10 to 12 minutes. Dust with icing (confectioners') sugar and serve immediately.
Cooking time: 1¼ hours
Serves 4

Cream Ice

METRIC/IMPERIAL	AMERICAN
2 egg yolks	2 egg yolks
50 g/2 oz icing sugar, sifted	½ cup sifted confectioners' sugar
2 teaspoons vanilla essence	2 teaspoons vanilla
300 ml/½ pint double cream	1¼ cups heavy cream
2 tablespoons milk	2 tablespoons milk

Turn the refrigerator to the coldest setting at least 1 hour before making the cream ice. Put egg yolks and sugar into a double saucepan (or heatproof basin standing over a saucepan of gently simmering water) and beat until thick and creamy. Remove from the heat. Continue beating the mixture until cool, then stir in the vanilla.

Pour the cream and milk into a chilled bowl and beat until lightly stiff. Gently fold in beaten yolks and sugar and then transfer to 1 or 2 ice cube trays, depending on size. Put into the freezing compartment of refrigerator and freeze for 45 minutes or until cream ice has frozen about 1 cm/½ inch around sides of tray. Turn into a chilled bowl, break up gently with a fork then stir until smooth. Return to washed and dried tray and freeze for 1½ to 2 hours or until firm.
Serves 4

Tortoni

METRIC/IMPERIAL	AMERICAN
150 ml/¼ pint double cream	⅔ cup heavy cream
150 ml/¼ pint single cream	⅔ cup light cream
25 g/1 oz icing sugar, sifted	¼ cup sifted confectioners' sugar
50 g/2 oz almond macaroons, finely chopped	¾ cup finely chopped almond macaroons
2 tablespoons Marsala or sweet sherry	2 tablespoons Marsala or sweet sherry
40 g/1½ oz ratafia biscuits, crumbled	⅔ cup crumbled ratafia cookies
2 egg whites	2 egg whites
a little melted chocolate	a little melted chocolate

Combine the creams and sugar and whisk together until softly stiff. Refrigerate for 1 hour. Stir the chopped macaroons, Marsala or sherry and half the crumbled ratafias into the chilled cream.

Whisk the egg whites until very stiff and fold into the cream mixture until smooth and evenly blended. Turn the mixture into a lightly oiled 1.25 litre/2¼ pint (6 cup) mould or large loaf tin (pan). Freeze until firm. Turn the Tortoni out of the mould and sprinkle with the remaining ratafia crumbs to coat. Decorate with melted chocolate, drizzled over the surface.
Serves 4

Cassata

METRIC/IMPERIAL	AMERICAN
600 ml/1 pint water	2½ cups water
150 g/5 oz dried skimmed milk powder	1⅔ cups dried skimmed milk powder
3 eggs	3 eggs
150 g/5 oz caster sugar	⅔ cup sugar
1 teaspoon vanilla essence	1 teaspoon vanilla
75 g/3 oz plain chocolate	3 oz semisweet chocolate
50 g/2 oz glacé cherries	¼ cup glacé cherries
25 g/1 oz dried mixed fruit	3 tablespoons dried mixed fruit
2 tablespoons sherry	2 tablespoons sherry

Whisk the water with the dried milk powder in a double saucepan or heatproof bowl standing over a saucepan of gently simmering water. Add the eggs, sugar and vanilla. Heat the custard gently, stirring continuously, until it is thick enough to coat the back of a wooden spoon; do not boil. Divide the custard into 2 separate freezer trays.

Shave some large curls of chocolate off the bar and reserve. Break the remaining chocolate into one of the freezer trays of hot custard and stir until melted. Place the freezer trays in the freezer for about 1 hour or until the custard begins to thicken.

Meanwhile chop the cherries and soak them with the dried fruit in the sherry.

Whisk both portions of half-frozen ice cream separately. Stir the fruit into the vanilla ice cream and return to the freezer. Measure half the chocolate ice cream into a 750 ml/1¼ pint (3 cup) loaf tin (pan). Level the surface and re-freeze. Keep the rest of the chocolate mixture cold. When the chocolate ice cream is sufficiently frozen, add the vanilla layer then finally the remainder of the chocolate ice cream. Leave to freeze hard.

To turn out, dip the pan quickly in hot water and invert onto a plate. Decorate the cassata with chocolate curls and serve cut into slices.
Serves 8

Cassata alla Siciliana

METRIC/IMPERIAL	AMERICAN
175 g/6 oz mixed glacé fruits (cherries angelica, pineapple, etc.)	1 cup mixed glacé fruits (cherries, angelica, pineapple)
1½ tablespoons maraschino liqueur	1½ tablespoons cherry liqueur
225 g/8 oz cottage cheese	1 cup cottage cheese
100 g/4 oz cream cheese	½ cup cream cheese
75 g/3 oz caster sugar	6 tablespoons sugar
8 trifle sponges	8 individual dessert sponge shells
Topping:	**Topping**:
175 g/6 oz plain chocolate, broken into pieces	6 squares (1 oz each) semisweet chocolate, broken into pieces
50 g/2 oz butter	¼ cup butter
1 egg	1 egg
175 g/6 oz icing sugar, sifted	1⅓ cups sifted confectioners' sugar
mimosa balls and angelica leaves, to decorate	mimosa balls and angelica leaves, to decorate

Chop the glacé fruits finely and put into a bowl with the liqueur. Sieve the cottage cheese and then mix well with the cream cheese and sugar. Split the sponges and use half of them to line the base and sides of a 1.2 litre/2 pint (5 cup) bowl. Stir fruits and liqueur into cheese mixture and turn into sponge-lined bowl. Arrange remaining slices of sponge over the top and chill, preferably overnight.

To make the topping: put chocolate and butter in a bowl over a pan of hot water and stir occasionally until melted. Beat the egg and mix it into the melted chocolate. Remove from the heat and beat in icing (confectioners') sugar. Invert dessert onto a serving plate and spread the topping over. Allow to set. Decorate with mimosa balls and angelica leaves. Serve chilled, cut into wedges with cream.
Serves 6

Galliano Cheesecake

METRIC/IMPERIAL	AMERICAN
Base:	**Base:**
150 g/5 oz plain flour, sifted	1¼ cups sifted all-purpose flour
50 g/2 oz caster sugar	¼ cup sugar
½ teaspoon salt	½ teaspoon salt
½ teaspoon grated lemon rind	½ teaspoon grated lemon rind
100 g/4 oz unsalted butter	½ cup unsalted butter
1 egg yolk	1 egg yolk
2 tablespoons Galliano liqueur	2 tablespoons Galliano liqueur
Filling:	**Filling:**
1 kg/2 lb ricotta or cottage cheese, sieved	4 cups ricotta or cottage cheese, sieved
4 eggs	4 eggs
100 g/4 oz caster sugar	½ cup sugar
25 g/1 oz plain flour	¼ cup all-purpose flour
4 tablespoons Galliano liqueur	4 tablespoons Galliano liqueur
2 tablespoons raisins, finely chopped	2 tablespoons finely chopped raisins
2 tablespoons mixed chopped peel	2 tablespoons chopped candied peel

To make the base: mix the flour, sugar, salt and lemon rind in a bowl. Rub (cut) in the butter until mixture resembles breadcrumbs. Mix in egg yolk and Galliano to form a dough. Press over base and up sides of deep 23 cm/9 inch loose bottomed cake tin (springform pan). Cook in a preheated moderate oven (180°C/350°F, Gas Mark 4) for 15 minutes until dry, but not browned.

To make the filling: blend the cheese, eggs, sugar and flour in a bowl. Stir in the Galliano, raisins and peel. Pour the filling into the cake tin (pan). Cook in a moderate oven (160°C/325°F, Gas Mark 3) for 1 hour. Remove cheesecake from cake tin (pan) and leave to cool on a wire rack.
Cooking time: 1¼ hours
Serves 6 to 8

Sicilian Cake

METRIC/IMPERIAL	AMERICAN
All-in-one-cake:	**All-in-one cake:**
225 g/8 oz soft margarine	1 cup soft margarine
225 g/8 oz caster sugar	1 cup sugar
4 eggs	4 eggs
225 g/8 oz self-raising flour, sifted with 2 teaspoons baking powder	2 cups self-rising flour, sifted with 2 teaspoons baking powder
grated rind of 2 oranges or 2 lemons	grated rind of 2 oranges or 2 lemons
Biscuits:	**Cookies:**
50 g/2 oz soft margarine	¼ cup soft margarine
75 g/3 oz plain flour	¾ cup all-purpose flour
25 g/1 oz sifted icing sugar	¼ cup sifted confectioners' sugar
Icing:	**Icing:**
2 egg whites	2 egg whites
450 g/1 lb sifted icing sugar	3½ cups sifted confectioners' sugar

Grease and base line a 25 cm/10 inch square cake tin (pan). Place all the cake ingredients in a bowl and beat with a wooden spoon for 2 to 3 minutes until well mixed. Turn the mixture into the tin (pan) and cook in a preheated moderate oven (160°C/325°F, Gas Mark 3) for 35 to 45 minutes. Turn out the cake onto a wire rack to cool and remove paper lining.

To make the biscuits (cookies): mix the soft margarine, flour and icing (confectioners') sugar in a bowl until the mixture forms a ball. Roll out thinly and cut out approximately 40 biscuits (cookies) with a heart-shaped cutter. Place on a lightly greased baking sheet and cook in a preheated moderate oven (180°C/350°F, Gas Mark 4) for about 10 minutes. Transfer the biscuits (cookies) to a wire rack to cool.

To make the icing: beat the egg whites and sugar together until smooth. Using a piping (pastry) bag fitted with a plain writing nozzle, pipe a lacy pattern on the top and sides of the cake and the tops of the biscuits (cookies). Place the cake on a large plate and arrange the biscuits (cookies) around the sides.
Cooking time: about 1 hour
Makes about 25 portions

Sicilian Cake
(Photograph: Stork Cookery Service)

Cold Zabaione

METRIC/IMPERIAL	AMERICAN
75 g/3 oz granulated sugar	6 tablespoons sugar
150 ml/¼ pint water	⅔ cup water
3 egg yolks	3 egg yolks
1 tablespoon Marsala	1 tablespoon Marsala
150 ml/¼ pint double cream, whipped	⅔ cup heavy cream, whipped

Dissolve the sugar in the water over a low heat, then boil until a thick syrup is formed. Gradually whisk the syrup into the egg yolks with the Marsala. Keep whisking until thick and creamy. Fold in the whipped cream and chill for 1 hour.
Cooking time: 15 minutes
Serves 3

Hot Zabaione

METRIC/IMPERIAL	AMERICAN
3 egg yolks	3 egg yolks
2 tablespoons caster sugar	2 tablespoons caster sugar
150 ml/¼ pint Marsala	⅔ cup Marsala

Put the egg yolks into a medium-sized heatproof bowl over a pan of simmering water. Add the sugar and Marsala and whisk until thick and creamy – about 8 minutes. Serve at once.
Cooking time: 10 minutes
Serves 3
Note: sweet sherry or Madeira can be used instead of Marsala, for making the hot or cold Zabaione.

Panettone

METRIC/IMPERIAL	AMERICAN
50 g/2 oz caster sugar	¼ cup sugar
25 g/1 oz fresh yeast	1 cake compressed yeast
150 ml/¼ pint lukewarm water	⅔ cup lukewarm water
3 egg yolks	3 egg yolks
1 teaspoon salt	1 teaspoon salt
400 g/14 oz strong plain white flour	3½ cups strong all-purpose white flour
100 g/4 oz butter, softened	½ cup soft butter
50 g/2 oz sultanas	⅔ cup raisins
50 g/2 oz seedless raisins	⅓ cup chopped candied peel
50 g/2 oz chopped mixed peel	2 tablespoons melted butter
25 g/1 oz butter, melted	

Stir 1 teaspoon of the sugar and all of the yeast into the water. Leave for about 10 minutes or until frothy.

Beat the egg yolks and stir in the yeast mixture, salt and remaining sugar. Beat in 225 g/8 oz (2 cups) of the flour and then gradually beat in the softened butter, a little at a time. Knead in the remaining flour.

Turn the dough onto a lightly floured surface and knead well until the dough is firm and elastic. Place in a lightly oiled polythene bag and leave in a warm place until doubled in size. Turn dough out onto a floured surface and knead in the sultanas, raisins and peel. Continue kneading until the fruit is evenly distributed. Place the dough in a greased 18 cm/7 inch round cake tin (pan). Cover with oiled cling film (plastic wrap). Leave in a warm place until dough has risen to top of tin (pan).

Remove cling film (plastic wrap). Brush with some of the melted butter and cook in a preheated moderately hot oven (200°C/400°F, Gas Mark 6) for 20 minutes. Reduce oven temperature to moderate (180°C/350°F, Gas Mark 4) and cook for a further 35 to 45 minutes. Remove from the tin (pan) and brush top and sides with remaining melted butter. Serve cut in thin wedges.
Cooking time: about 1 hour
Serves 10

Easter Dove Bread

METRIC/IMPERIAL	AMERICAN
15 g/½ oz fresh yeast, or 2 teaspoons dried yeast and 1 teaspoon caster sugar	½ cake compressed yeast, or 2 teaspoons dried yeast and 1 teaspoon sugar
150 ml/¼ pint warm milk	⅔ cup warm milk
1 egg, beaten	1 egg, beaten
1 teaspoon vanilla essence	1 teaspoon vanilla
275 g/10 oz strong plain white flour	2½ cups strong all-purpose flour
1 teaspoon caster sugar	1 teaspoon sugar
pinch of salt	pinch of salt
grated rind of ½ lemon	grated rind of ½ lemon
25 g/1 oz butter	2 tablespoons butter
Glaze:	**Glaze:**
1 egg white, lightly beaten	1 egg white, lightly beaten
1 tablespoon caster sugar	1 tablespoon sugar

Blend the fresh yeast into the milk or dissolve the sugar in the milk and sprinkle on the dried yeast. Leave in a warm place for about 10 minutes or until frothy. Beat in the egg and vanilla.

In a large bowl, combine the flour, sugar, salt and grated lemon rind. Rub (cut) in the butter. Beat the yeast liquid into the flour to form a firm dough. Turn onto a lightly floured surface and knead for 10 minutes until the dough is firm and no longer sticky. Place the dough in a large bowl and cover with lightly oiled cling film (plastic wrap). Leave to rise until double in size and springy to the touch – about 1 hour in a warm place or 1½ to 2 hours at average room temperature.

Uncover and turn dough onto a lightly floured surface. Knead dough for 2 minutes until smooth and firm. Divide dough in half. Roll out one piece into an oval measuring 25 × 5 cm/10 × 2 inches. Place on a greased baking sheet and flatten out ends of oval. Roll remaining dough into a triangle measuring 13 cm/ 5 inches at the base and 25 cm/10 inches at each side. Arrange the triangle over the oval of dough to form a cross shape. Pinch the dough triangle just above and below the oval to form the head and body of the "dove". Elongate the tip of the triangle to form the beak. With a knife, score the tail and wings to look like feathers.

Cover with lightly oiled cling film (plastic wrap) and leave to rise until bread has increased in size slightly.

Uncover "dove" and brush with egg white. Sprinkle sugar over wings and tail. Cook in a preheated moderate oven (160°C/325°F, Gas Mark 3) for 50 to 55 minutes until browned. Remove bread and place carefully on a wire tray. Serve warm with butter.
Cooking time: 50 to 55 minutes
Serves 8 to 10

Sweet Pizza

METRIC/IMPERIAL	AMERICAN
Pastry:	**Dough:**
225 g/8 oz plain flour	2 cups all-purpose flour
pinch of salt	pinch of salt
100 g/4 oz margarine	½ cup margarine
cold water	cold water
Filling:	**Filling:**
4 tablespoons honey	4 tablespoons honey
50 g/2 oz chopped walnuts	½ cup chopped walnuts
1 teaspoon mixed spice	1 teaspoon ground allspice
50 g/2 oz chopped mixed peel	⅓ cup chopped candied peel
To finish:	**To finish:**
1 tablespoon warmed honey	1 tablespoon warmed honey
25 g/1 oz chopped walnuts	¼ cup chopped walnuts

Sift the flour and salt into a bowl and rub (cut) in the margarine until the mixture resembles breadcrumbs. Add sufficient cold water to make a dough. Roll out the dough thinly on a lightly floured surface into a rectangle. Spread the honey over the dough and sprinkle with the walnuts, spice and peel. Roll up the dough into a long sausage shape.

Brush the roll with warmed honey and sprinkle with walnuts. Make cuts along the roll at 2.5 cm (1 inch) intervals. Cook in a preheated moderate oven (180°C/350°F, Gas Mark 4) for 25 minutes.
Cooking time: 25 minutes
Serves 4

Quick Snack Meals

Tomato and Salami Pizza

METRIC/IMPERIAL
Scone base:
225 g/8 oz self-raising
flour
1 teaspoon baking
powder
½ teaspoon dry
mustard
½ teaspoon salt
50 g/2 oz soft
margarine
½ teaspoon dried
mixed herbs
7 tablespoons milk
Topping:
100 g/4 oz grated
cheese
100 g/4 oz sliced
salami
2 tomatoes, sliced
½ teaspoon dried
oregano
2 slices ham, cut into
strips
parsley sprigs

AMERICAN
Scone base:
2 cups self-rising flour
1 teaspoon baking
powder
½ teaspoon dry
mustard
½ teaspoon salt
¼ cup soft margarine
½ teaspoon dried
mixed herbs
7 tablespoons milk
Topping:
1 cup grated cheese
¼ lb sliced salami
2 tomatoes, sliced
½ teaspoon dried
oregano
2 slices ham, cut into
strips
parsley sprigs

Sift together the flour, baking powder, mustard and salt, add the margarine, herbs and milk and mix with a wooden spoon to form a dough. Knead lightly and roll into a 23 cm/9 inch round. Place on a greased baking sheet.

Sprinkle with the cheese and arrange salami and tomatoes on top. Sprinkle on herbs, and arrange a lattice of ham strips on top. Cook in a moderately hot oven (200°C/400°F, Gas Mark 6) for 20 to 25 minutes. Garnish with parsley.
Cooking time: 20 to 25 minutes
Serves 4 to 6

Tomato and Salami Pizza
(Photograph: Stork Cookery Service)

Pan Pizza

METRIC/IMPERIAL
100 g/4 oz plain flour
pinch of salt
1 teaspoon baking
powder
4 tablespoons water
3 tablespoons oil
chopped parsley
Topping:
1 × 113 g/4 oz packet
liver pâté
1 × 227 g/8 oz can
tomatoes, drained
and chopped
50 g/2 oz beer
sausage
50 g/2 oz haslet
50 g/2 oz Cheddar
cheese, grated
25 g/1 oz grated
Parmesan cheese

AMERICAN
1 cup all-purpose
flour
pinch of salt
1 teaspoon baking
powder
4 tablespoons water
3 tablespoons oil
chopped parsley
Topping:
¼ lb packet liver pâté
1 × 8 oz can
tomatoes, drained
and chopped
2 oz beer sausage
2 oz haslet
½ cup grated
Cheddar cheese
¼ cup grated
Parmesan cheese

Sift the flour into a bowl, make a well in the centre and add the salt, baking powder and sufficient water to make a fairly firm dough. Knead for a few minutes, then roll out into a thin round about 18 cm/7 inches in diameter.

In a heavy frying pan, heat the oil and, when hot, add the pizza base. Cook for 5 minutes or until the underside is golden brown, turn the base over. Spread the pâté over the base and cover with the tomatoes. Cut the meats into strips, arrange these on the tomatoes and cover with the cheeses. Cover the frying pan with a lid and cook for approximately 10 minutes, or until the cheese is melted. Brown quickly under a hot grill (broiler) and sprinkle with chopped parsley.
Cooking time: 20 minutes
Serves 2 to 3

Tomato, Olive and Salami Pizza

METRIC/IMPERIAL	AMERICAN
Topping:	**Topping:**
1 × 800 g/1 lb 12 oz can tomatoes	1 × 1 lb 12 oz can tomatoes
1 onion, chopped	1 onion, chopped
2 tablespoons tomato purée	2 tablespoons tomato paste
2 teaspoons dried oregano	2 teaspoons dried oregano
1 teaspoon sugar	1 teaspoon sugar
salt and freshly ground pepper	salt and freshly ground pepper
175 g/6 oz Mozzarella cheese, sliced	6 oz Mozzarella cheese, sliced
100 g/4 oz salami, sliced	¼ lb salami, sliced
50 g/2 oz stuffed green olives	½ cup stuffed green olives
1 tablespoon grated Parmesan cheese	1 tablespoon grated Parmesan cheese
Scone base:	**Scone base:**
225 g/8 oz self-raising flour	2 cups self-rising flour
1 teaspoon baking powder	1 teaspoon baking powder
1 teaspoon salt	1 teaspoon salt
25 g/1 oz softened butter	2 tablespoons softened butter
150 ml/¼ pint milk	⅔ cup milk
2 tablespoons French mustard	2 tablespoons Dijon-style mustard

To make the topping: put the tomatoes with their juice, onion, tomato purée (paste), oregano and sugar into a pan and season with salt and pepper. Cook gently for about 30 minutes without a lid to reduce the mixture to a thick pulp. Adjust seasoning to taste.

Meanwhile make the scone base: sift the flour, baking powder and salt into a large bowl. Rub (cut) in the butter and mix to a soft dough with the milk. Turn onto a large floured baking sheet, then roll out to a 25 cm/10 inch round. Spread mustard over the pizza base.

When the tomato mixture is cooked, spread it over the dough to within 2.5 cm/1 inch of the edge. Arrange Mozzarella, salami and halved olives on the tomato mixture, and sprinkle with Parmesan cheese.

Cook in a preheated moderately hot oven (200°C/400°F, Gas Mark 6) for about 30 to 40 minutes until well risen and golden brown.
Cooking time: 1 to 1¼ hours
Serves 6 to 8

Pizza with Sprats (Smelts)

METRIC/IMPERIAL	AMERICAN
Base:	**Base:**
225 g/8 oz self-raising flour	2 cups self-rising flour
pinch of salt	pinch of salt
50 g/2 oz butter	¼ cup butter
7 tablespoons cold water	7 tablespoons cold water
Topping:	**Topping:**
1 tablespoon olive oil	1 tablespoon olive oil
1 onion, chopped	1 onion, chopped
1 clove garlic, crushed	1 clove garlic, crushed
1 × 227 g/8 oz can tomatoes	1 × 8 oz can tomatoes
1 tablespoon tomato purée	1 tablespoon tomato paste
1 teaspoon dried mixed herbs	1 teaspoon dried mixed herbs
salt and freshly ground black pepper	salt and freshly ground black pepper
100 g/4 oz button mushrooms, sliced	1 cup sliced button mushrooms
450 g/1 lb sprats, washed and drained	1 lb smelts, washed and drained
100 g/4 oz Cheddar cheese, grated	1 cup grated Cheddar cheese

Sift the flour and salt into a bowl and rub (cut) in the butter until the mixture resembles fine breadcrumbs. Add enough cold water to make a soft dough. Roll out to a 30 cm/12 inch round. Place on a greased baking sheet.

Heat the oil in a frying pan and sauté the onion and garlic until just browned, add the tomatoes with their juice, tomato purée (paste), herbs and salt and pepper to taste. Simmer for 5 minutes, then allow to cool. Spread the cooled tomato mixture on the base, then add half the mushrooms. Arrange the sprats (smelts) on top, radiating from the centre. Top with the remaining mushrooms and cheese and season to taste.

Cook in a preheated hot oven (220°C/425°F, Gas Mark 7) for 15 minutes, then reduce the heat to 200°C/400°F, Gas Mark 6 and cook for a further 20 to 25 minutes until cooked. Serve cut in slices with a mixed salad.
Cooking time: ¾ to 1 hour
Serves 4 to 6

Pizza Margherita

METRIC/IMPERIAL	AMERICAN
15 g/½ oz fresh yeast, or 2 teaspoons dried yeast and 1 teaspoon sugar	½ cake compressed yeast, or 2 teaspoons dried yeast and 1 teaspoon sugar
300 ml/½ pint warm water	1¼ cups warm water
450 g/1 lb strong plain white flour	4 cups strong all-purpose white flour
2 teaspoons salt	2 teaspoons salt
15 g/½ oz lard	1 tablespoon shortening
1 × 800 g/1 lb 12 oz can tomatoes	1 × 1 lb 12 oz can tomatoes
225 g/8 oz Mozzarella or Bel Paese cheese	½ lb Mozzarella or Bel Paese cheese
1 teaspoon dried basil olive oil	1 teaspoon dried basil olive oil

Dissolve the fresh yeast in 150 ml/¼ pint (⅔ cup) of the warm water. Or dissolve the sugar in the same amount of warm water and sprinkle the dried yeast on top. Leave the yeast in a warm place for 10 minutes or until frothy.

Mix the flour and salt in a bowl and rub (cut) in the lard (shortening). Add the yeast liquid and remaining water to make a soft dough. Knead the dough until smooth, firm and elastic and the dough leaves the bowl clean. Shape dough into a ball. Put to rise in a large greased bowl. Cover lightly with greased cling film (plastic wrap) until the dough doubles in size and springs back when pressed with a floured finger. This process will take: 45 to 60 minutes in a warm place; 2 hours at room temperature; 12 hours in a cold room or larder; 24 hours in a refrigerator.

Meanwhile prepare any extra topping ingredients of your choice – see suggestions below.

Turn the risen dough onto a board and flatten it with the knuckles or a rolling pin into a long strip. Brush with oil and roll up like a Swiss (jelly) roll. Repeat this 3 times in all. Divide dough into 6 pieces and shape each piece into a thin 23 cm/9 inch round. Place on greased baking sheets. Drain the tomatoes and mash them almost to a pulp. Spread the tomatoes over each pizza. Cut the cheese into slices and place on the tomatoes, then add any extra topping ingredients. Sprinkle with basil and then pour over a little olive oil. Cook in a preheated hot oven (230°C/450°F, Gas Mark 8) for 20 minutes.

Extra Pizza Topping Suggestions

METRIC/IMPERIAL	AMERICAN
175 g/6 oz salami, sliced	6 oz sliced salami
50 g/2 oz anchovy fillets	2 oz anchovy fillets
50 g/2 oz black olives	½ cup ripe olives
1 tablespoon capers	1 tablespoon capers
100 g/4 oz mushrooms, sliced	1 cup sliced mushrooms
1 onion, cut into rings	1 onion, cut into rings

Cooking time: 20 minutes
Serves 6

Pizza Flan

METRIC/IMPERIAL	AMERICAN
Pastry:	**Dough:**
175 g/6 oz plain flour	1½ cups all-purpose flour
¼ teaspoon salt	¼ teaspoon salt
40 g/1½ oz lard	⅓ cup shortening
40 g/1½ oz margarine	
1 egg, beaten	1 egg, beaten
Filling:	**Filling:**
1 tablespoon olive oil	1 tablespoon olive oil
1 onion, sliced	1 onion, sliced
100 g/4 oz liver sausage	¼ lb liver sausage
50 g/2 oz Cheddar cheese, grated	½ cup grated Cheddar cheese
100 g/4 oz bratwurst sausage	¼ lb bratwurst sausage
2 tomatoes, sliced	2 tomatoes, sliced
¼ teaspoon dried mixed herbs	¼ teaspoon dried mixed herbs

Sift the flour and salt into a bowl and rub (cut) in the fat until the mixture resembles fine breadcrumbs. Stir in the beaten egg and mix to a dough. Roll out the dough to a 23 cm/9 inch round and fold up the edges.

Heat the oil in a pan and fry the onion until soft.

Spread the liver sausage over the flan base and cover with the onions and cheese. Grill (broil) the bratwurst until evenly browned then cut into strips. Arrange the bratwurst and tomato slices attractively on the flan. Sprinkle with the herbs. Cook in a preheated hot oven (220°C/425°F, Gas Mark 7) for 30 to 35 minutes.
Cooking time: 45 minutes
Serves 4

Wholewheat Pizza

METRIC/IMPERIAL	AMERICAN
15 g/½ oz fresh yeast or	½ cake compressed
1½ teaspoons dried	yeast or
yeast and	1½ teaspoons dried
½ teaspoon sugar	yeast and
6-7 tablespoons warm	½ teaspoon sugar
milk	6-7 tablespoons warm
225 g/8 oz	milk
wholewheat flour	1 cup wholewheat
salt and pepper	flour
25 g/1 oz butter	salt and pepper
Topping:	2 tablespoons butter
1 onion, chopped	**Topping:**
50 g/2 oz streaky	1 onion, chopped
bacon, chopped	¼ cup chopped
1 tablespoon olive oil	bacon
75 g/3 oz cooked ham,	1 tablespoon olive oil
chopped	⅓ cup chopped
450 g/1 lb spinach	cooked ham
pinch of nutmeg	1 lb spinach
½ teaspoon lemon	pinch of nutmeg
juice	½ teaspoon lemon
225 g/8 oz tomatoes	juice
100 g/4 oz Mozzarella	1 cup sliced tomatoes
cheese, sliced	¼ lb Mozzarella
¼ teaspoon dried	cheese, sliced
oregano	¼ teaspoon dried
	oregano

Dissolve the fresh yeast in the warm milk. Or dissolve the sugar in the warm milk and sprinkle the dried yeast on top. Leave the yeast in a warm place for 10 minutes or until frothy.

Mix together the flour and a little salt and pepper and then rub (cut) in the butter. Make a well in the centre and pour in the yeast mixture. Stir well until the mixture forms a ball. Knead on a lightly floured surface for 5 minutes. Place dough in an oiled polythene bag and leave in a warm place for 1 hour until doubled in size.

Meanwhile fry the onion and bacon in the oil until tender and add the cooked ham. Cool. Wash the spinach thoroughly and remove the stalks. Cook the spinach for 2 minutes in boiling water seasoned with the nutmeg, garlic salt and lemon juice. Drain thoroughly and cool.

Turn the dough onto a lightly floured board and knead again for 1 minute. Roll out to a 28 cm/11 inch round and place on an oiled baking sheet. Cover the base with the spinach, add the bacon, onion and ham. Top with the sliced tomatoes and cheese and sprinkle over the herbs. Cook in a preheated moderately hot oven (200°C/400°F, Gas Mark 6) for 25 minutes.
Cooking time: 45 minutes
Serves 6

Italian Pancakes

METRIC/IMPERIAL	AMERICAN
Filling:	**Filling:**
40 g/1½ oz butter	3 tablespoons butter
2 onions, chopped	2 onions, chopped
350 g/12 oz minced beef	1½ cups ground beef
1 teaspoon Wor-	1 teaspoon Wor-
cestershire sauce or	cestershire sauce
Yorkshire relish	3 tablespoons tomato
3 tablespoons tomato	ketchup
ketchup	**Batter:**
Batter:	1 cup all-purpose
100 g/4 oz plain flour	flour
pinch of salt	pinch of salt
1 egg	1 egg
300 ml/½ pint milk	1¼ cups milk
Cheese sauce:	**Cheese sauce:**
25 g/1 oz butter	2 tablespoons butter
25 g/1 oz plain flour	¼ cup all-purpose
300 ml/½ pint milk	flour
salt and pepper	1¼ cups milk
100 g/4 oz grated	salt and pepper
Cheddar cheese	1 cup grated Cheddar
25 g/1 oz grated	cheese
Parmesan cheese	¼ cup grated
	Parmesan cheese

Melt the butter in a pan and lightly fry the onions. Add the meat and stir until lightly browned. Add the Worcestershire sauce and ketchup and cook, covered, for 30 minutes.

Meanwhile make the pancake batter: sieve the flour and salt into a bowl, add the egg and half the milk and beat until smooth. Gradually stir in the remaining milk. Heat a very little fat in a 20 cm/8 inch frying pan and pour in enough batter to make a thin layer over base of the pan. Cook until the underside is golden, then turn to cook other side. Turn onto greaseproof (waxed) paper and keep warm on a plate over a pan of hot water. Make 7 more pancakes.

Divide the filling between the pancakes and roll up. Place the pancakes in a greased shallow ovenproof dish and keep warm.

To make the cheese sauce: melt the butter in a pan, add the flour and cook for 1 minute. Remove from the heat and gradually stir in the milk. Return to the heat and bring to the boil, stirring. Cook for 1 minute, remove from the heat, add seasoning and grated Cheddar cheese, and stir until cheese has melted. Pour the sauce over the pancakes. Sprinkle over Parmesan and brown under the grill (broiler).
Cooking time: 1 hour
Serves 4

Italian Pancakes
(Photograph: Hammonds Sauce Company Limited)

Mortadella Omelette

METRIC/IMPERIAL	AMERICAN
2 tablespoons olive oil	2 tablespoons olive oil
350 g/12 oz potatoes, coarsely grated	3 cups coarsely grated potatoes
1 onion, finely chopped	1 onion, finely chopped
50 g/2 oz stuffed green olives, sliced	½ cup sliced stuffed green olives
2 tomatoes, skinned and chopped	2 tomatoes, peeled and chopped
1 green pepper, cored, seeded and diced	1 green pepper, seeded and diced
100 g/4 oz mortadella sausage, diced	½ cup diced mortadella sausage
3 eggs	3 eggs
salt and freshly ground pepper	salt and freshly ground pepper

Heat the oil in a large frying pan, add the potatoes and onion and cook gently for 10 to 15 minutes until the mixture is golden brown. Add the remaining ingredients, except the eggs, and cook for a further 4 minutes.

Beat the eggs and salt and pepper together and add to the frying pan. Cook the omelette until set and brown underneath. Invert the omelette onto a plate, slide the omelette back into the pan and cook the underneath. Serve with French bread and a salad.
Cooking time: 30 minutes
Serves 4

Salami and Vegetable Omelette

METRIC/IMPERIAL	AMERICAN
40 g/1½ oz butter	3 tablespoons butter
1 small onion, sliced	1 small onion, sliced
1 red pepper, cored, seeded and sliced	1 red pepper, seeded and sliced
175 g/6 oz salami, chopped	6 oz salami, chopped
1 × 213 g/7½ oz can red kidney beans, drained	1 × 7½ oz can red kidney beans, drained
salt and freshly ground pepper	salt and freshly ground pepper
4 eggs	4 eggs
1 teaspoon dried mixed herbs	1 teaspoon dried mixed herbs

Melt the butter in a pan and fry the onion and pepper until softened. Stir in the salami, beans and salt and pepper to taste and heat through.

Lightly beat the eggs together with the herbs and pour over the vegetables. Cook gently, forking up the cooked mixture frequently to let the raw egg mixture run to the bottom of the pan. When nearly firm all over, fold the omelette in half, cut in two and serve.
Cooking time: 15 minutes
Serves 2

Noodle Omelette

METRIC/IMPERIAL	AMERICAN
75 g/3 oz noodles	¾ cup noodles
salt and freshly ground pepper	salt and freshly ground pepper
2 eggs, beaten	2 eggs, beaten
pinch of nutmeg	pinch of nutmeg
40 g/1½ oz butter	3 tablespoons butter
1 small onion, sliced	1 small onion, sliced
2 tomatoes, skinned and sliced	2 tomatoes, peeled and sliced
1 × 5 cm/2 inch piece cucumber	1 × 2 inch piece cucumber
75 g/3 oz Cheddar cheese, grated	¾ cup grated Cheddar cheese

Cook the noodles in boiling salted water for 10 minutes. Drain and cool. Mix the noodles with the eggs, salt, pepper and nutmeg to taste.

Melt half the butter in an 18 cm/7 inch frying pan and cook the onion until soft but not browned. Add the tomatoes. Peel and slice the cucumber and add to the frying pan. Cook gently for 1 minute. Remove from the pan and keep hot.

Melt the remaining butter in the pan and pour in the egg and noodle mixture. Cook to lightly brown the underside. Place the cooked onion, tomatoes and cucumber on top, season and sprinkle over the grated cheese. Place under a hot grill (broiler) until lightly browned. Serve hot.
Cooking time: 30 minutes
Serves 2

Crostini

METRIC/IMPERIAL	AMERICAN
8 small round slices bread	8 small round slices bread
8 slices Cheddar or Bel Paese cheese	8 slices Cheddar or Bel Paese cheese
50 g/2 oz anchovy fillets	2 oz anchovy fillets
50 g/2 oz olives, sliced	½ cup sliced olives

Toast the bread on both sides. Place slices of cheese on top and grill (broil) until just melted. Remove from the heat and arrange strips of anchovy and sliced olives on top. Serve hot.
Cooking time: 10 minutes
Serves 4

Focaccia

METRIC/IMPERIAL	AMERICAN
25 g/1 oz fresh yeast, or 15 g/½ oz dried yeast and 1 teaspoon sugar	1 cake compressed yeast, or 1 tablespoon dried yeast and 1 teaspoon sugar
450 ml/¾ pint warm water	2 cups warm water
1 kg/2 lb strong plain white flour	8 cups strong all-purpose white flour
2 teaspoons salt	2 teaspoons salt
150 ml/¼ pint olive oil	⅔ cup olive oil
3 onions, thinly sliced	3 onions, thinly sliced
1 egg	1 egg
100 g/4 oz black olives	¾ cup ripe olives

Dissolve the fresh yeast in 150 ml/¼ pint (⅔ cup) warm water. Or dissolve the sugar in the same amount of warm water and sprinkle the dried yeast on top. Leave the yeast in a warm place for 10 minutes or until frothy.

Sift 225 g/½ lb (2 cups) flour into a bowl with the salt. Add the yeast mixture and 3 tablespoons oil and mix to a soft dough. Knead dough until smooth, firm and elastic – about 5 minutes. Shape dough into a ball. Put dough to rise in a large greased bowl, covered lightly with greased cling film (plastic wrap) until it doubles in size (about 1 hour).

Meanwhile fry the sliced onions gently in 3 tablespoons oil until tender but not browned; cool.

When the dough has doubled in size, sift the remaining flour into a separate bowl, make a well in the centre and add the egg, remaining 4 tablespoons oil and remaining 300 ml/½ pint (1¼ cups) warm water. Mix well together then add the risen dough. Turn out onto a board and knead for 5 minutes. Return to the greased bowl and cover with the greased cling film (plastic wrap). Leave to rise for 45 minutes.

Divide dough in half. Roll to a 5mm/¼ inch thickness and use to line two baking sheets 30 cm × 23 cm/12 × 9 inches. Spread over the cooked onions and oil. Add the olives, brush generously with extra oil and cook in a preheated hot oven (220°C/425°F, Gas Mark 7) for 30 minutes. Serve hot or cold, on its own or with a sliced tomato salad.
Cooking time: 1 hour
Makes 16 slices
Sliced Tomato Salad: slice tomatoes, sprinkle with salt, sugar and oregano. Pour over some olive oil and chill. Spoon some tomato salad on top of each slice of warm focaccia.

Wholewheat Mortadella Scones

METRIC/IMPERIAL	AMERICAN
100 g/4 oz self-raising flour	1 cup self-rising flour
100 g/4 oz whole-wheat flour	1 cup wholewheat flour
1½ teaspoons baking powder	1½ teaspoons baking powder
50 g/2 oz margarine	¼ cup margarine
50 g/2 oz mortadella sausage, diced	¼ cup diced mortadella sausage
150 ml/¼ pint milk	⅔ cup milk

Mix the flours and baking powder together. Rub (cut) in the margarine and mix in the mortadella. Pour in the milk and mix lightly to form a fairly soft dough. Roll out on a lightly floured surface to 1 cm/½ inch thickness.

Using a 5 cm/2 inch cutter, cut out approximately 12 scones. Place on a greased baking sheet and brush with milk. Cook in a preheated hot oven (220°C/425°F, Gas Mark 7) for 10 to 12 minutes. Serve warm.
Cooking time: 12 minutes
Makes 12

Tuna Pizza

METRIC/IMPERIAL	AMERICAN
Base:	**Base:**
1 teaspoon paprika pepper	1 teaspoon paprika pepper
1 × 275 g/10 oz packet white bread mix	1 × 10 oz packet white bread mix
2 tablespoons tomato purée	2 tablespoons tomato paste
200 ml/⅓ pint hot water	⅞ cup hot water
Topping:	**Topping:**
1 large onion, sliced	1 large onion, sliced
1 tablespoon olive oil	1 tablespoon olive oil
1 × 198 g/7 oz can tuna, drained	1 × 7 oz can tuna, drained
175 g/6 oz Cheddar cheese, grated	1½ cups grated Cheddar cheese
salt and freshly ground black pepper	salt and freshly ground black pepper

Add the paprika pepper to the bread mix. Blend the tomato purée (paste) in the hot water and add it to the bread mix. Follow packet instructions up to the point for kneading for 5 minutes.

Roll out the dough to a 30 cm/12 inch round and place on a greased baking sheet. Lightly fry the sliced onion in the olive oil and spread over the dough. Cover with flaked tuna and grated cheese. Add salt and pepper to taste and cook in a preheated hot oven (220°C/425°F, Gas Mark 7) for 20 minutes.
Cooking time: 30 minutes
Serves 4

Savoury Mushroom Tart

METRIC/IMPERIAL	AMERICAN
225 g/8 oz frozen puff pastry	½ lb frozen puff pastry
450 g/1 lb macaroni	4 cups macaroni
3 tablespoons olive oil	3 tablespoons olive oil
1 teaspoon salt	1 teaspoon salt
175 g/6 oz chicken livers, chopped	¾ cup chopped chicken livers
225 g/8 oz mushrooms, sliced	2 cups sliced mushrooms
2 onions, thinly sliced	2 onions, thinly sliced
4 eggs, beaten	4 eggs, beaten
salt and freshly ground pepper	salt and freshly ground pepper
50 g/2 oz grated Parmesan cheese	½ cup grated Parmesan cheese
25 g/1 oz butter	2 tablespoons butter

Roll out the pastry and use to line a 1 litre/2 pint pie dish. Cook the macaroni in a large pan of boiling water with 1 tablespoon oil and 1 teaspoon salt until tender. Drain and add the chopped chicken livers.

Heat the remaining oil in a pan and fry the mushrooms and onions, then add them to the macaroni mixture with the eggs. Add salt and pepper to taste and pour into the lined pie dish. Cover with grated Parmesan cheese and knobs of butter. Cook in a preheated hot oven (220°C/425°F, Gas Mark 7) for 30 to 40 minutes, or until top is well browned. Serve with fresh tomato sauce (see page 44) and Parmesan cheese.
Cooking time: 1 hour
Serves 4 to 6

Index

The publishers would like to acknowledge the following
photographers – Robert Golden: pages 2 & 3, 22; Eric Carter:
page 27; Graham T. Langridge: page 30; Theo Bergstrom:
pages 35, 38, 43, 51 & 59.
Illustrations by Susan Neale.